Choice Words
for Local Marketers

How to Use Content Marketing
to Generate Revenue

Susan Anderson

Choice Words for Local Marketers

Copyright © 2013 by Susan Anderson

For those who dare to create.

A1067

Same muse.

Table of Contents

Who Are You, and Why Should You Read This Book?

> *Who are you*
> *Who who who who*
> *Who are you*
> *Who who who who*
>
> **The Who, Who Are You**

OK. I got that out of my system. After titling this chapter, it happened again. As a writer, getting lyrics stuck rattling around in my brain is an occupational hazard. Now you get to finish the song. I'll wait.

Oh crap. You may be too young to even KNOW that song. Go home and YouTube it, young Padawan.

Anyhow...

I wrote this book for you.

Don't believe me? Let's see how well I nail who you are. You're a local online marketer. By definition, you're new to this business, because this is a new business. You've probably just sat through a seminar on how to make money in this business – maybe in person, maybe through a video course, and quite possibly through a video course I helped develop.

You're probably sold on the idea of using outsourcers to do all the backlink building, directory submission, and other tedious tasks required to help your clients dominate the search engine results page so they ultimately get more customers and make more money. Those are tasks you don't want to do yourself, any more than you'd like to poke your eyeballs with a pencil.

You get it, that outsourcing that stuff is the only way you can ratchet up your capacity. Outsource, and you can handle all the clients you want, all at a profit as you mark up the cost of the outsourcing. Do it all yourself, and you can probably handle no more than 1.3 clients. It's time-consuming, it's boring, and it's not where the money is. You're better off spending your time meeting with clients and prospects, creating strategies for helping your clients edge out their competitors online, growing your own knowledge base, and developing your mindset as a successful business owner.

Seeing as you've probably just sat through a couple of days, or weeks (or days that felt like weeks – how's that tailbone?)

of training, why on earth would you want to sit and read this book?

Well, know how that outsource team is your ticket to succeeding as a local online marketer without chaining yourself to your desk to build links?

It's the same idea as the SEO outsourcing, but for content creation. We're talking everything from website content to press releases, blogging, whitepapers, case studies, newsletters, articles, videos, ebooks, and email marketing messages.

This book will show you how to get all the high-quality content you'll need for your own business and for your clients, AND how you can make content creation a profit center for your business. You'll also learn a little about the most commonly published content pieces, why your clients need them, and how to sell words at a nice profit.

Hate writing? Too bad. Your clients are probably expecting you to write for their sites.

Love writing? Too bad, again. Because writing isn't where you'll make your money, unless you're really good and want to become a freelance writer. (In which case, I've got a whole different book for you to read – *Working Writer,*

Happy Writer: How to Build a Thriving Writing Business from NOTHING.)

See, even if you're a great writer, right now you shouldn't be. Your focus should be on consulting with your clients and reselling the services they need to market their business, get new customers, keep their doors open, and grow companies that are thriving.

They need content. You just shouldn't be the one creating it. And for the love of all that's good, THEY should not be creating it, either.

The King Is Dead, Long Live the King

You only have to be in local online marketing for about 78 seconds to hear, "Content is king." It's true, but boy have the particulars changed over the past 43 minutes. See, Google's top-secret algorithms have changed dramatically over the years. Used to be you could literally copy and paste a list of keywords into a website page, change the font color to match the background, and rank instantly for those search terms. Counts as content, sort of.

Then, ranking became a contest of who could out-publish whom. Didn't matter if the content was total vomit-inducing crap – all that mattered was that it was published and had a backlink to the client's website.

Spinners and overseas writers were the best friend of Internet marketers everywhere. Until Google said, "MMMmmmmm, nope." Slap! Into the sandbox with you.

We need to clarify what we're talking about regarding content.

Will content alone guarantee multiple listings on a search engine results page? Nope.
Is it quantity over quality? Of course not.
Should you scrap content creation altogether because it's not the silver bullet it used to be for traffic generation? Silly question.

See, even if content never got you a single new website visitor (and that's just absurd), you STILL need great content for your site and your clients' sites. Content builds credibility, helps prospects know, like, and trust a business, shortens a sales cycle, prompts visitors to become customers, and keeps visitors on a website long enough that the search engines take notice and say, "Hmmm, apparently this site is good enough for people to stay a while, let's bump them up the list a bit, why don't we?"

That Settles It. But Now You're Wondering…
You're convinced. I see your head nodding. You get it: content… good, writing it yourself… bad.

So how do we do this thing?

How do you get all the content you need for yourself and your clients, make money on every word you deliver, and never have to write a single syllable yourself?

Glad you asked.

Mind you, you've got lots of content creation companies out there. While I sure hope we'll be a good fit to work together, I'm also just hoping this book will give you an understanding of what's possible, and how to go out there and get it.

That said, all I can do is tell you how my firm, Triumph Communications, works.

There are three ways to work this:
Triumph is invisible.
In this scenario, we're a white label provider for you. As far as your clients are concerned, you pulled content out of the air, your own brain, or your in-house team. You do all the interacting with your client, then pass along the information we need. We bill you. You bill your client.

Triumph is your content creation department.

We work under your brand. If you need us to interact with your clients, we'll do so as part of your team. Sometimes the best way to get information is for someone to interview your clients; we can be that someone. Again, we bill you; you bill your client.

Triumph is your preferred provider.

For this one, you're following the business model of being a consultant who's got the scoop on a great content creation resource, which you share with your clients. We'll communicate directly with them, and can either bill you or bill them.

Questionnaires Out the Wazoo

By now you've heard the advice to systematize your business and to create process documents and checklists so you can achieve consistent results.

We did that.

Of course, I didn't know to do that back in the dark ages of my business. And by dark ages, I mean 2005, when I started writing professionally – just me and about 1,732 SEO articles about custom t-shirt designs. Do anything that many times, and you'll get a system, too.

Anyhow, the biggest challenge in writing for someone's business is the brain dump. How do my clients get what they know, how they speak, and all the details that go into effective writing from their brain into mine, and back in written form?

Questionnaires and intake forms. We're constantly tweaking and improving ours, and it's made an amazing difference in the end result.

The Money Thing

Way back in 2005 when I started Triumph, I soon became legendary. See, I had this superhero-like ability to under-price everything I did. It was almost like there was a money allergy or something. My mentor, before thwacking me in the head and throwing my secret stash of Nutella down a city sewer, had some wise words: "You're doing it wrong! You're not supposed to PAY your clients. They're supposed to pay YOU!"

Details.

Yeah, now all you can think about is why you didn't find Triumph back then!
Water under the bridge.

So here's how we do this. It may be a little different from what you're used to. We price everything flat rate, rather than based on time. This is because I don't think writing fast should be a crime. The best copy and content I ever write just flows – fast. Also, by giving you a flat rate, you know exactly what a project will cost… rather important as you resell our content creation services.

We also do payment up-front. What? Yeah. I don't chase money. It's distracting and distraction leads to sucky writing. See, in some ways, I'm operating a service business. You're my client – in that, you fall under my protection and guidance, and you get some space in my writers' brains even when we're not actively working on your project. But in some ways, I'm selling products – articles, press releases, website content, etc. People pay up-front for products. (Free advice for you – read "Built to Sell". Not right now, of course… finish this book first. But after you read that one, you'll understand.)

Now, there's some really good news in here for you. You probably got your hot little hands on this book because you're somehow connected with Kevin Wilke. I've got a soft spot in my heart for that guy, and his students. Because I was one, long before I ever became VP Design and Development (content creator!) at Nitro. If you've got the chance, ask Kevin about how his "Website Marketing Do-Over" video contest netted him a friend and content writer. Anyhow… Kevin and I were talking about how important it is for you, as a local online marketer, to have access to a trustworthy source of excellent content for your own business, and for your clients. You could definitely go out and assemble a team of writers, although from personal experience, I've got to tell you it's not easy. But if you want to skip that step and just get content, here's your chance.

If you order content through
www.TriumphCom.com/nitro
…you'll get the best pricing we offer. You get great content at a fair price; I get clients who share my passion for helping local businesses thrive, no matter what the economy is doing. By helping these businesses succeed, you're also benefiting their employees and vendors, their customers and communities, and all of the families of everyone involved. By working with you, I get the satisfaction of knowing I'm helping them all a little, too.

Alright. Enough mushiness.

Here's what you need to know to get the most value from reading this book:
It's divided into the most frequently-ordered content deliverables local online marketers use.

With each kind of content, you'll get an explanation of what the content is, why it's useful, why your clients need this, how it can go sideways if not done right, how to sell it at a profit, and some particulars about getting this project done with Triumph.

You want to think of each service in two ways – How would your business benefit from getting this kind of content? And, how would you and your clients benefit if you re-sell it to them?

My hope is that you'll enjoy the read. I'm not ashamed to admit I cracked myself up writing it, to the point my dog became disgusted with the giggling and went to another room to resume licking himself without distraction. My test readers liked it, too – although they kind of had to, or risk being asked to handle the revisions themselves.

Of course, I'd also like to do business with you if we're a good fit.

GOT A HOLE
in
YOUR BUCKET?

Good Website
Content Preserves the
Prospect Pipeline

BY
SUSAN ANDERSON

Choice Words

Got a Hole In Your Bucket?
Good Website Content Preserves the Prospect Pipeline

As a local online marketer, your prime directive is this: Use the Internet to deliver prospective customers to your clients' hot little hands.

You've either mastered the laundry list of tasks involved in traffic generation and SEO, or been wise enough to out-source that never-ending job to a good team. Smart!

But here's the thing, and there's always a thing.

Generating all the website traffic in the world won't do your client a bit of good if when that traffic hits the client's site, they uniformly say, "Ehhhh" - or worse. That's a hole in the bucket, and all those leads will leak through your hands rather than streaming into the profit reservoir you're building.

Website content should suck. It should suck visitors into a time warp where they stay on your client's site longer than they ever intended to, wandering into its deepest pages because they just can't stop consuming the content they find there.

As if that weren't enough, you also want to have your keywords in the text, too, because that will help with search engine results page placement. However, winning favor with the search engines is tricky. You can't just shove keywords into every nook and cranny of text and expect good results. The writer has to focus first on your site visitors' experience. Take good care of them, provide truly valuable information, and make them want to take action on what they read, and you've got the start of winning website content. Put the people first, and the bots will follow suit if you follow best practices for keyword placement.

Semantics First: What is Website Content?
Let's make sure we're on the same page (oh yes, the puns are free). What we're talking about on this project is words appearing on a web page. Technically videos, forms, audio files and graphics on a page are website content, too. All we're looking at right now is written content, designed to encourage people to stay on the website, learn more about a product or service, and then take action.

Correctly optimized web content will attract the attention of search engines and increase the likelihood your client's website will show up for your chosen keywords. While there's never any guarantee the search engines will reward your site with traffic for hitting the moving target of proper keyword placement, by focusing on high-quality content and best practices for keyword usage, you've got the best shot at getting traffic from search engines. By creating the right kind of web content, you can help your clients get the exposure they need.

Website content should be written in a way that's persuasive, engaging, and SEO-friendly. The goal is to meet the needs of human readers and search engines alike.

The ROI on Website Content

You're convinced. Now let's talk about what you need to communicate to your clients so they happily order website content from you.

Here's a short list of benefits your client receives by having excellent website content. Website content…

• Increases traffic to your site
• Increases conversions on every page
• Increases your Google Page Rank, helping you get more and higher listings on the results page
• Helps your prospects know, like, and trust you more
• Shortens your sales cycle as prospects educate and persuade themselves by reading your content
• Works as a great pre-sell

On the other hand, poorly written website content can do some serious damage. Poorly written content kills credibility and goes over like a sack of cement with Google. Here are a few ways website content creation can go sideways:

- Keyword spamming – hated by all readers, human and otherwise.
- Duplicate content – the speediest way to create content is to steal it! Of course, there are repercussions.
- Grammatical and spelling errors – Nothing gets traffic running away from a site faster.
- Jargon jungle – Make your prospects feel like they stumbled into an industry training conference, and they'll hate every one of the few seconds they spend trying to decipher your acronyms and insider lingo.
- Leave them hanging – Even good content, if it has no call to action, results in nothing happening.

How to Re-Sell Website Content Services to Clients

1. Every website owner needs professionally-written content. Here's how you recognize a good prospect for this service:
- When you find website content that looks like the business owner (or a pre-teen nephew) did the writing.

- When you encounter prospective clients with websites that function like online business cards – not much more than contact information.
- When the content reads like the most boring textbook you've ever had to suffer through.
- When there are typos and grammatical errors that make the site owner look stupid.
- When there's so much jargon and industry-insider lingo that you feel stupid.
- When you find yourself mentally saying, "Words, words,words" as you pretend to read because actually reading the text seems like a perfect waste of a few minutes of your life.
- When, after reading, you have no idea why you should care, or what you're supposed to do next.

2. Ask probing questions to assess their need, and help them to see it, too:

- How confident do you feel that the text on your website is working to make your prospective customers know, like, and trust you?
- How thoroughly does your existing website content explain what makes your business different from your competitors, describe the products or services you sell, detail who you serve and how you work?
- Who wrote the content on your website?

- How often do your customers mention that your website helped them decide to do business with you?
- When was your website content written? Has it been updated since then?

3. Use a checklist to analyze their current website content with them:

- Content consists of short, easy-to-read sentences, each focused on a single idea.
- Paragraphs are short. No more than 3-5 sentences each.
- Website content is 350-700 words long.
- Content includes white space to make text easy for readers to skim, scan, and scroll and get the information they need.
- Text includes subheadings to break information into sections.
- Text includes bullet points or numbered lists.
- Text is written at about the 8th grade reading level.
- Text uses action words to engage the reader.
- Each page includes a powerful call to action that spells out the next steps a reader should take.
- Each page includes anchor text that links it to other relevant pages on the site.

4. Communicate the benefits of professionally written website content. High quality, fresh web content can help them make more money by:

- Drawing the regular attention of the search engines, since relevant, updated content is irresistible to them.
- Keeping their website visitors coming back for more.
- Positioning them as experts in their fields.
- Compelling visitors to take action.
- Shortening the sales cycle as visitors self-serve the information they need to make a buying decision.

5. Present a selection of website content creation packages.

- Create your own website content creation packages by adding a margin to the packages of an outsource team.
- Give each package a name. You will find that if you offer three package levels, most clients will choose the middle package.
- Add this service into your marketing materials.
- Add website content creation to the list of services on your own website.
- Order website content for your client.
- Simply go to www.TriumphCom.com/nitro to order.

- Choose your package.
- Pay via PayPal.
- We will contact you to confirm receipt of your order and send you a questionnaire to complete on behalf of your client.
- If you prefer, for an additional fee, we can interview you or your client to extract that information (painless, we promise!) without you having to complete the questionnaire.
- We'll draft the text based on that information, and send to you for approval within a week or less, in most cases.
- If revisions are needed, just let us know, and we'll get them done and back to you quickly.

Sample Text for Your Website

You might want to include some website copy on your own site to let you clients and prospects know you can provide website copy for their sites. Many business owners assume their web development consultant can provide copy – and they're usually wrong. If your prospects have been shopping around, they may have resigned themselves to thinking they'll have to create their own website text. You can delight them by taking that task off of their shoulders and getting it done for them painlessly.

Want Your Website to Do More than Just Look Good? The Right Words Turn Your Site into Your Best Salesperson

More than the images and layout on your website, the words you choose can either send it to the top of the search engines, or leave it buried on page 43 where your prospective customers will never find it. Writing web contents is a specialized skill that combines search engine optimization, wordsmithing, and gentle persuasion. A well-written site can:

- Win favor with the most popular search engines, which means your site appears higher in the search results.
- Drive more sales. Higher search engine placement = more visitors = more sales.
- Give you a competitive edge over other businesses. Your site positions you as THE expert in your field.
- Shorten your sales cycle. Your prospects get the information they need to make a buying decision before they even call.

To learn more about how you can turn your website into a sales generation tool just by using the right words, click or call today.

Look, you're working hard – or paying good money – to generate website traffic and top placements for your clients. The newly boosted traffic numbers look great on those reports you're showing off. But without good content, if your client's site is turning prospects off, that traffic just won't convert. Short-term, clients are happy with just a spike in traffic; what they really want is more business.

Fresh and well-done. That's how website content works.

Blogging is the One-Two Punch

WIN SOME LOVE FROM THE BIG G

HOW ONLINE MARKETERS CAN PROFIT FROM OUTSOURCED BLOGGING SERVICES

SUSAN ANDERSON

Choice Words

Win Some Love from the Big G: How Online Marketers Can Profit from Outsourced Blogging Services

Ever known someone who had to have the last word? It's possible Google added some last word weight into its algorithm. Most searches bring up results that show when the page was published. Maybe it's some sort of content expiration date, reinforcing that fresh is best.

Blogging is about the simplest way to go big with a website. Every post adds a new page, enlarging the site's online footprint. Every post gives prospects more insight into the company, helping them know, like, and trust them more. Every post gives Google more reason to consider your client's site an authority, nudging them toward the top of the search engine results page.

Semantics First: What is Blogging?

Alright, sometimes this segment is going to seem so obvious you'll wonder why it made its way into this book. However, you'd be surprised how often people have a whole 'nuther idea about what some content projects are, what they do for a business, and how to use them to generate revenue.

Blog posts can be anywhere from a few paragraphs to a page long or more, but most bloggers try to go for 200 to 600 words. This length allows for enough detail about the topic without overwhelming the reader.

The content of a blog post should be helpful to the reader, even if it's on a corporate or small business blog. No reader wants to sit down and read through a totally promotional piece of sales literature. Strive to provide helpful information and advice. Helpful information will keep the readers coming back and it will also increase the likelihood that other sites will link to the posts.

For readability, keep sentences and paragraphs short. People can't absorb large chunks of text on the screen and are most likely to absorb the content if it's written in manageable chunks. For most blogs, the writing should clock in at about the 8th grade reading level.

We get questions about blogging all the time, and here are the ones we get the most:
- Isn't this just like article marketing?
- Why Do Businesses Need a blog?
- So, just post on Blogger, right? Since Google owns it, that sounds good… right?
- My client's a subject matter expert – how can someone else write for this business?

- Wouldn't it be better if my clients blogged for themselves?
- Does blogging really make a difference with search engine ranking?

Isn't Blogging Just Like Article Marketing?

Well, blog posts are like mini articles, but article marketing involves submitting articles to article directories – as many as possible. Article marketing is definitely still a valuable tactic, but there are a few hitches with it. Articles have to adhere to the directories' editorial guidelines, which usually forbid links in the body. You get 1-2 links in the resource box, but that's it. Also, the text itself has to adhere to editorial guidelines – only using the keyword or its derivatives a certain number of times, and using third person language, for example.

With blogging, you have complete editorial control. You can say whatever you want, however you want, as many times as you want. You (or your client) own the publishing platform, so there's no danger of the post being rejected.

Why Do Businesses Need a Blog?

Sometimes business owners object to the term 'blog' because they're remembering back to the early days of the Internet when the blogging landscape was marked by posts about what bloggers ate for breakfast, soapbox speeches, or conspiracy theories. No wonder they turn their noses up at the idea of a blog for their business!

So, call it an article page.

We'll get into the benefits more in detail in a bit, but here are a few: search engine favor, credibility building, traffic generation, sales cycle shortening, and connection-building.

Post to Blogger, Right?
No.

The logic is there – win favor with Google by posting on Google-owned properties. It's part of the theory behind posting videos to YouTube, and it makes sense there. Blogging is different, though. It's important to post blogs on a site you control – not on one that could disappear faster than you can say "Google Knol" (http://knol.google.com/faq).

With videos, you're doing distribution on multiple video sharing sites, and you own the video and have the file stored somewhere else. If YouTube goes down, you're covered. Plus, YouTube's the biggest video site out there – Blogger is not typically considered a destination site.

The Subject Matter Expert (SME)

True, in most businesses, it would be hard to write with the level of knowledge and experience the owner has accumulated. Good thing that's not necessary!

The funny thing with SMEs is that sometimes they get so riled up about their industry that they go on and on, not realizing they've lost their audience. An experiment for you: start a conversation with an SME at the next cocktail party you go to. Then try to change the subject. [insert evil laugh here… you're stuck!]

Prospects usually aren't experts. They're approaching the subject from a beginning knowledge level and don't want to be blown out of the water by advanced concepts, terminology, and industry insider info and debates. They want the basics. Because of that, it's almost best if the blog writer doesn't know squat about the topic at the start of the project. They'll likely have the same questions a prospect would have. As they research the topic, they'll be just a few steps ahead of the prospect – and that's far more engaging than listening to an SME drone on and on.

Shouldn't Your Clients Blog for Themselves?

………. OK. Sorry. I just had to compose myself, getting a grip after cackling maniacally. It's okay; breathing again.

Sure, that would be great. In their spare time. With their spare brain cells. On a regular schedule (and no, once a quarter doesn't count as 'regular'). Following best practices for blogging. Oh, and with good grammar and spelling, and an engaging writing style.

See the problem(s)?

I run into clients all the time who say, "I'd like to tackle the blogging on my own." You can nearly set your watch to three days, 6 hours, and 17 minutes when they're back, saying maybe they'd like us to handle blogging for them after all.

It's happened enough that I've come up with the perfect compromise. How about this? The SME can blog as often as they like! Whenever they feel inspired, just pop out a blog post! Yay, SME!!!

Meanwhile, we'll handle the regular blogging. We'll be sure there are posts being written and published every week, every day, or at whatever frequency you want. We can even write under a specified name for the business, so there's no need to worry if we don't quite capture the SME's voice.
That brings us to a great solution you can offer those clients who insist on having SME-level posts published. The brain dump between subject matter expert and the writer can

happen with a recorded interview. In just a few minutes of talking with your client, an interviewer (can be you, or can be us – whatever you prefer) can get all the info needed to write a blog post from your client's perspective, using their wording.

Does Blogging Help with SEO?

Like luring a stray cat to your front porch day after day, publishing fresh content to your blog brings Google's bots back for a sniff. Because the content is good, and statistically likely to be the latest bit written on your keyword, Google will serve it up to people searching for information using that keyword phrase. So, yes.

Mind you, blogging is not a silver bullet. We won't be brazen enough to proclaim you're guaranteed top spots for blog posts. There's a lot that goes into search engine results page placement – and we don't even know exactly what Google's looking for in the top placements. However, it sure can't hurt, if it's done well. Wonderful side benefits include adding girth to your client's site, engaging prospects with information that's valuable to them, maintaining the appearance that your client's is a thriving business, and increasing the perception that your client is an expert with information to share.

Here are some other random and lovely blogging statistics, courtesy of HubSpot)

- Blog frequency impacts customer acquisition. 92% of companies who blogged multiple times a day acquired a customer through their blog. (HubSpot State of Inbound Marketing, 2012)
- The global population of blog readers keeps growing. (eMarketer, August 2010)
- 81% of marketers rated their blog as useful or better. (HubSpot State of Inbound Marketing, 2012)
- There are 31% more bloggers today than there were three years ago. (eMarketer, August 2010)
- 46% of people read blogs more than once a day. (HubSpot Science of Blogging 2010)
- Most people read 5-10 blogs. (HubSpot Science of Blogging, 2010)
- Nearly 40% of US companies use blogs for marketing purposes. (eMarketer, August 2010)

The ROI on Blogging

There's one major reason your clients will pay you to provide blogging services for them. Keeping a blog updated is a total pain in the butt. Here are just a few big challenges you'll take off your clients' plates if you get their blogs taken care of for them:

- What should I write about? They may find it difficult to come up with topics to write about in the first place.

- Keyword goes WHERE? They probably lack effective SEO skills, so even if they write their own blog posts, their efforts are unlikely to please both the search engines and their website visitors.

- I keep meaning to get around to it! They're busy running their business. Finding time to regularly update a blog is not likely to be a priority long-term

- I hate writing. Really, really, REALLY hate it. Not being professional writers, their lack of writing skills may prove to be a deficit when it comes to promoting and maintaining their image as an expert.

- Aw man... but I blogged last week! Blogs are always hungry. Constantly adding new content to a blog is the only way for it to be effective, yet that requires a sizeable commitment.

Blogs are only effective if they are maintained and updated regularly. Given the option of having someone else do this for them, many business owners will recognize the time and money savings outsourcing this task represents.

Different types of blog post clients will find different payoffs from having a well-maintained and constantly updated blog. A few suggestions you can make to help your clients get the maximum benefit from their blogs:

- Use your clients' blogs to announce and promote seasonal or holiday specials to their customers. Provide a promotional code they can use to get access to the special.

- Consider running Pay Per Click ads on your client's blog to monetize it. Anytime a blog reader clicks one of the ads, your client will receive anywhere from a few cents to a few dollars, depending on the niche.

- After your client's blog grows to have a substantial readership, it's very possible companies will contact you about running their banner ads on the blog for a monthly fee.

- There may be affiliate products (ebooks, physical products, and services) that your client would like to recommend to readers. If you register your client as an affiliate, there will be a commission every time readers purchase through a link on the blog.

- Use the blog to survey your client's customers. Just by asking a great question, you can get valuable market research right from your client's target market.

- Include a subscription box on your client's blog to build an email list of prospects and customers you can market to in the future.
- Link to your clients' blogs from their social media sites, like Facebook, Twitter, and LinkedIn.

How to Re-Sell Blogging Services to Clients

1. Every website needs a blog. Every blog needs posts. Here's how you recognize a good prospect for this service:
- When you find websites that have no blog.
- When you find blogs that haven't published in the past month or so.
- When you find blogs written by the business owner.

2. Ask probing questions to assess their need, and help them to see it, too:
- How often do you add content to your website's blog?
- Who writes blog posts for you?
- How much time do you or your staff spend creating blog posts?
- How far in advance does your editorial calendar go for your blog?

3. Use a checklist to analyze their current blog with them:
- Posts publishing a minimum of once per week.

- Engaging title that makes you want to click and read.
- Paragraphs are short. No more than 3-5 sentences each.
- Posts are 200-600 words long.
- Posts include white space to make text easy for readers to skim, scan, and scroll and get the information they need.
- Posts include subheadings to break information into sections.
- Posts include bullet points or numbered lists.
- Posts are written at about the 8th grade reading level.
- Posts use action words to engage the reader.
- Each post includes a powerful call to action that spells out the next steps a reader should take.
- Each post includes an image that further engages a reader's attention.

4. Communicate the benefits of professionally written blog posts. Regular blogging can help them make more money by:

- Drawing the regular attention of the search engines, since fresh, relevant content is irresistible to them.
- Keeping their website visitors coming back to see what's new.
- Positioning them as experts in their fields.

- Compelling visitors to take action.
- Shortening the sales cycle as visitors self-serve the information they need to make a buying decision.

5. Present a selection of done-for-you blogging packages.
- Create your own blogging packages by adding a margin to the packages of an outsource team.
- Give each package a name. You will find that if you offer three package levels, most clients will choose the middle package.
- For blogging packages, you could make either the frequency of posts or the source of the info (is an interview involved?) the distinguishing mark between pricing levels.
- Add this service into your marketing materials.
- Add done-for-you blogging to the list of services on your own website.

6. Order blogging services for your client. Simply go to www.TriumphCom.com/nitro to order.
- Choose your package.
- Pay via PayPal.
- We will contact you to confirm receipt of your order and send you a questionnaire to complete on behalf of your client.
- If you prefer, for an additional fee, we can interview you or your client to extract that information (pain-

less, we promise!) without you having to complete the questionnaire.

- We'll create an editorial calendar for the month's posts for your approval.
- We'll draft the text based on what you've approved, and send to you for final approval within a week or less, in most cases.
- If revisions are needed, just let us know, and we'll get them done and back to you quickly.
- We can post the blogs for your client, set to publish at whatever interval you prefer. The more competitive the niche, the more frequently blogs should publish.

Sample Text for Your Website

Want a Simple Way to Make Google Love Your Site and Build a Loyal Client Base without Advertising?
Online, content is king. Google and the other search engines are constantly looking for what's new. By having a fresh, updated blog as part of your business website, you get:

- Increased exposure for your business 24/7, so your customers can find you when they're ready to buy
- A shorter selling cycle because your prospects can get more information about your products and services before their first contact with you

- A more favorable position in the search engine results, which means more website visitors, and ultimately more profits for your business
- Easy advertising revenues
- A boost in your credibility and authority in your business from frequent online publishing

However, everything that makes a blog so powerful also makes it time-consuming and challenging to do right. Effective blogs are updated a few times a week following best practices in search engine optimization. Leave your blog sitting stagnant, and it won't do a thing to help your business.

Successful business owners understand the value of out-sourcing this time-consuming but vital task. By partnering with a local online marketing consultant, you get all the benefits of a dynamic, current blog without the hassle and time expense of writing it yourself.

Click or call today to find out how easy it is to have a professional, powerful blog working for your business.

Blogging doesn't have to leave you feeling like you're tasked with feeding an insatiable fire-breathing beast. Get all of the benefits of publishing regularly – adding mass to your website, building credibility, cutting the sales cycle down to size, and winning favored placement on the search engine results pages.

Publish well; publish often; publish painlessly.

PROMOTE and PROTECT

Using Press Releases in Local SEO

By Susan Anderson

Choice Words

Promote and Protect: Using Press Releases in Local SEO

Press releases are one of the most powerful ways to build your clients' online presence. Google LOVES them. By nature, they're high-quality content (just the facts - no promotion), and in most cases press releases are reviewed and approved by a human editor.

Most business owners completely ignore press releases as part of their marketing strategy because they don't think they've got news to share, they're still stuck in thinking of traditional media, and they don't know how to do a good press release.

As far as having news to share, pretty much anything going on in your client's business can be turned into a newsworthy event. Do a quick Google search on reasons to send a press release, and you'll find hundreds of happenings your clients could use for ideas. It doesn't have to be earth-shattering news - just news.

Semantics First: What Are Press Releases?
Press releases are different from nearly every other piece of content you get created for your clients:

- These are news pieces. You can't have salesy language at all - just the facts.
- They cover the who, what, where, when, why, and how to get a complete story.
- They use neutral and impersonal language. This is different from blog posts and articles, where you can be more personable. A press release shouldn't have first- or second-person pronouns in it. The only exception is in the quote segment, which features an expert, a company representative, a customer, someone like that. This quote is the only place in the whole press release that can be slightly promotional, opinionated, or personal. It's also the only part that can include a first- or second- person pronoun.
- It's got to have a strong headline that compels someone to read the release.
- For each press release, feature one of your keywords. It should appear in the headline, the summary, early in the first sentence, and then sprinkled throughout the release where it fits naturally.

You'll need to submit your press releases to press release distribution sites in order to get any results.

Why Do Businesses Need Press Releases?

Over the years, it's hit me that press releases are rather misunderstood. Lots of people confuse them with bids to get local media coverage. Truth is, as far as traditional media goes, the odds of your press re-lease leading to a newspaper article, TV spot, radio interview, or anything even close to that are slim.

That's not the point.

There are two primary reasons for issuing press releases: promotion and protection. The point of the promotional press release is to get some of the highest quality backlinks available by publishing online. You're not at the mercy of a journalist or print publisher who's got space restraints and needs to sell papers - publishing a press release online is much, much easier. Of course, you can submit your press releases to traditional media outlets and hope for the best - in some cases your story will get picked up. But don't focus on that.

The second way you can help your clients is in building a hedge of protection around their online reputation. If you provide online reputation monitoring, management, or repair, you know all it takes is pissing off someone who knows how to blog, build a site, or take out a PPC ad to succeed with an online smear campaign against your client.

All your hard work in helping your client become more visible online kind of circles the drain when this is what the results bring up:

"[YOUR CLIENT] sucks. They stole my money, bit my dog, and ate all the Nutella!"

Play along. You get the idea.

This kind of link building is a little different. Normally, you're aiming to rank for keywords people use to search for your client's products or services. With these protective press releases, it's all about claiming valuable search engine results page territory for your client's name and business name. By publishing before there's ever an online reputation challenge, you may just prevent it from ever happening.

Now, that's forward thinking! Of course, many business owners won't do that. They'll wait until they have a disgruntled former employee, grumpy customer, or crush gone bad who decides to exact vengeance online.

You're still covered.

It'll cost your client more when you move from online reputation management to repair. A lot more. As in hundreds of dollars to distribute each press release, and doing it weekly until the trolling stops. PRWeb, you will find, is exceptionally good at distribution. Within hours of your press release going live there, your press release will dominate the truly dedicated to out-publishing you, it should work.

Do Press Releases Help with SEO?

In case you weren't paying attention to every word of my glorious prose above, the answer is: YES. But with a caveat. If you've ever lived in the northeast, you know one thing about snow: It falls and then it stays all winter. Literally, in April you could be slip-sliding on the same (now filthy) snow that fell in October and got covered by all the subsequent storms in between.

Now, if you've ever lived in Colorado (at least where I did), the opposite is true. You could get a foot and a half dumped on you on Wednesday, and be walking on bare grass by the end of the day Friday.

Press release distribution can quickly blanket your client's info all over the search engine results pages. But it doesn't last – at least not usually.

I'm not SEO geek enough to find out where all the press release links eventually go, but they do go somewhere. The first days and weeks after a major blast out to all the press release distribution sites, and you're the talk of the town (or at least you're dominating the search results for your headline). Then all of a sudden, POOF! Gone.

Hey, I didn't make the Google machine. I just write for it. To get traction with press releases, you've got to do them regularly.

The ROI on Press Releases

While a single press release is likely to generate good results for a while, it's far more effective to make press releases a regular part of your marketing strategy for your clients. This is easy to do if you will help them create an editorial calendar, planning 1-2 press releases per month. Much like how a magazine schedules its issues a year or more in advance, any business can create a rough plan for press releases based on its calendar.

Help your client create an editorial calendar by reviewing their annual calendar (either the upcoming year, or if that's not available, look at last year's calendar and see which events are likely to repeat). Look for anything that seems newsworthy:

- New product or service
- New website or approach

- New book or publication
- Opening of a new branch
- Announcing a joint venture, partnership
- Offering availability for speaking, free information
- Sponsoring an event, award, or seminar
- Attending advanced training
- Announcing a contest, fundraiser, or other charitable involvement
- and much more

Also be sure to look for ways you can connect your clients with current events. Your client could comment on a news story, the results of a study, a public policy discussion, or local event.

In case your stomach just lurched at the idea of having to create an editorial calendar, don't fret. We can do that.

A few more tips you need, no matter who does your press release writing:

Timing Matters
For press releases that are tied to a current event, timing is especially important. If the press release is issued too late, the media has lost interest – if it is issued too soon before an event, nobody will have a clue what you're talking about.

Call to Action

Without sounding hypey or promotional, include a call to action in every press release. Consider what prospects should do as a next step after reading the information, then use a call to action that nudges them to take that next step. For example, if the press release announces a new product, provide information about where it is sold. If the press release announces that your client is offering a free consultation, provide directions on how a reader can schedule it.

No Jargon

Make your press release readable to the average person, not just industry insiders. Avoid jargon, acronyms, and technical terms. If insider language can't be avoided, be sure to provide a definition of the term when it is first introduced.

No HTML

Online press release distribution sites generally prohibit HTML in the body of a press release. In general, anchor text or links are also not allowed.

An Active Voice Wins

Avoid using passive verbs in your writing, and especially in a press release. Passive verbs are not only wordier, but they lack punch and are harder to read. As you write, it's almost always better to say what you need to say in fewer words.

Powerful verbs are an effective way to convey the message in a way that keeps readers reading.

How to Re-Sell Press Release Services to Clients

1. Every business needs press releases. Every press release needs distribution. Here's how you recognize a good prospect for this service:

   - When you find business owners who have exciting news to announce.
   - When you find business owners who aren't issuing press releases on a regular basis.
   - When you find clients struggling with an online reputation challenge, or who want to avoid ever having one.

2. Ask probing questions to assess their need, and help them to see it, too:

   - How often do you send out press releases?
   - Who writes press releases for you?
   - How do you get them distributed online?
   - How much time do you or your staff spend creating and publishing press releases?
   - How far in advance does your editorial calendar go for your press release campaign?

3. Use a checklist to analyze their current press release plan and past press releases with them:

- Press releases published a minimum of once per month.
- Does each release have an engaging headline that makes you want to click and read?
- Each press release includes a powerful call to action that spells out the next steps a reader should take.
- Each press release is manually submitted to a list of 25+ quality distribution sites.

4. Communicate the benefits of professionally written press releases. Regular distribution can help them make more money by:

- Drawing the regular attention of the search engines, since fresh, relevant content is irresistible to them.
- Potentially getting some attention from local media.
- Positioning them as experts in their fields.
- Subtly compelling readers to take action.
- Building credibility – the perception is that only 'real' businesses use press releases.
- Shortening the sales cycle as visitors self-serve the information they need to make a buying decision.
- Present a selection of done-for-you press release packages.

5. Create your own press release packages by adding a margin to the packages of an outsource team.

- Give each package a name. You will find that if you offer three package levels, most clients will choose the middle package.

- For press release packages, you could make the frequency of writing and distribution, the quantity of submissions, or the source of the info (is an interview involved?) the distinguishing mark between pricing levels.

- Add this service into your marketing materials.

- Add done-for-you press releases to the list of services on your own website.

6. Order press release services for your client. Simply go to www.TriumphCom.com/nitro to order.

- Choose your package.

- Pay via PayPal.

- We will contact you to confirm receipt of your order and send you a questionnaire to complete on behalf of your client.

- If you prefer, for an additional fee, we can interview you or your client to extract that information (painless, we promise!) without you having to complete the questionnaire.

- We can even create an editorial calendar for orders of six or more press releases for your approval.

- We'll draft the text based on what you've approved, and send to you for final approval within a week or less, in most cases.

- If revisions are needed, just let us know, and we'll get them done and back to you quickly.

- We can handle distribution for you with our resource who will submit to 25+ press release sites, or even post to PRWeb.com for you, if you buy a distribution package there.

Marketing Tips

Go for Regular Clients Who Need Online Reputation Management

A one-off press release may put money into your bank account, but if you can establish regular press release clients who are ordering one or two press releases each month, you will create a steady stream of income. The best way to turn one press release gig into an ongoing assignment is to help your clients create an editorial calendar. This eliminates the need for them to remember to order more press releases. Because there is a cumulative effect that happens with issuing regular press releases, your client will begin seeing better results and will connect their increased exposure with your press releases.

Offer a Free Consult

Many business owners know that press releases are something they should be doing, but have no idea how to write them or even what they'd issue a press release about in the first place. In a free consultation, you could explain the benefits of issuing regular press releases and help the client by brainstorming some possible story angles. More than likely, they will ask you to handle writing and submitting the press release because in the course of the consultation, they will share so much information that it will be easy for you to carry the project to completion.

Offer Distribution Services

For business owners, only half the battle is getting the press release written. Without distribution, it is nearly useless. Distribution is not hard, but it can be done incorrectly, leading to poor results. The process of distribution is tedious and for a client who lacks the resources to do it correctly, it seems like an overwhelming task. Offer packages that include the writing and the distribution so your clients' experience is pain-free, easy, and has the best chances of getting the results they desire.

Sample Text for Your Website

Need to Get the Word Out About Your Business? What's Cheaper than Advertising and Ten Times More Effective?

Press releases are the secret weapon of successful marketing firms. Delivering a one-two publicity punch, a powerfully written press release can attract positive media attention and send a stream of highly-targeted traffic to your website.

Just imagine what would happen if your business was mentioned in the evening news, featured in the local paper in connection with a current event, or if you were interviewed on a daily talk show. It's exposure like this that money (almost) can't buy.

Some tips for running an effective press release campaign:

- Submit your press release to online distribution sites to get powerful search engine optimization benefits.
- Send your press release to the right people at the right media outlets locally for the best chance of having your story picked up.
- Be sure to follow all the best practices for writing press releases to ensure your press release is picked up rather than sent to the trash file.

- Remember the importance of your press release headline – you have only about three seconds to grab the attention of your readers.
- Send press releases 1-2 times a month for maximum results.

A professionally written press release can position you as an industry expert, generate local and national media interest, and increase your website traffic all at the same time.

To discover how to use professional press releases to promote your business, click or call today for a free consultation.

Press releases allow you to outplay, outlast, and out-publish your competitors and detractors, so they're excellent tools to use as you protect your clients. Done well, and done regularly, they've also got SEO juice that can't be beat.

Susan Anderson

what are they
READING
in the john now?

Newsletters Make a Comeback

Choice Words

What Are They Reading in the John Now? Newsletters Make a Comeback

Remember when it used to be so exciting to get an e-newsletter? You might have even paid for some subscriptions. You gave out your name and email address like you were entering a raffle or something. Back then, it was even exciting to get spam emails. You'd click them and think maybe, just maybe you did have a long-lost relative in Nigeria who died without an heir, and named you his only successor and the inheritor of his gajillion dollar estate.

Marketers went bananas, too.

The biggest, best advice sounded a little like the line from Fried Green Tomatoes except the secret wasn't in the sauce, it was in the list. "Build a list, build a list, build a list," they sang as a chorus. Great advice, actually, and newsletters were the golden ticket for building that list, the ethical bribe prospects lined up to get.

And then email became a chore.
I used to chuckle when my ex-husband complained that he had gotten "like a dozen emails today". Clearly he had not subscribed to Warrior Forum, gotten himself onto all the top Internet marketing gurus' lists, or subscribed to

FlyLady.net to try to regain some semblance of neat and clean in the house. Dozens? I actually pay Google for extra space in my gmail account (also known as my filing cabinet).

But I digress.

Point is, now people kind of want to puke when they think about how much email is accumulating. Therapists soothe their clients saying, "Hey, your inbox will be full the day you die. It's okay."

So while an email newsletter is still something, it's not everything.

It's common for your recipients, even if they're truly interested in reading the latest issue, to save it for "later".

And by later, I mean never.

Meanwhile, back in your mailbox out by the road, you're almost kind of wishing someone would send you a letter. But a newsletter would do, too. After all, you've now got no reading material for your bathroom. You get something in the mail that's even remotely interesting-looking, you save it from the ruthless over-the-trashcan sorting session, and it gets safely ensconced… on the back of the toilet. Depending on your roughage intake, it might take you a few days to get through it, but you actually read it. And if it's good, you read every word.

That, my friends, is my poop theory of publishing. You can share it. I don't mind.

And by 'theory' I mean that my creative partners and I nearly came to blows over this one, and since I'm writing this book, you're hearing my preference for print first. We had a knock-down, fangs-bared kind of discussion (Okay, that's a lie. It was spirited, but friendly… just seemed more dramatic if we'd rolled up sleeves and brandished fists. Play along, okay?)

In one corner, some were throwing out statistics showing that digital newsletters were still THE way to go… and that print is the crutch of the ill-informed throwback. In the other corner were some saying that even though we have no hard data to back it up, anecdotal and personal experience lead us to predict a return to print for a while… until the pendulum swings back again, or onto something entirely new. We, in the print corner, believe we're not behind the times, but that we've looped the space-time continuum and are now trendsetting. Or something.

In the end, we compromised. I'll share the list of pros and cons for print and digital formats in a bit. What's best for you and for your clients depends on some particulars. You'll be best suited for helping them decide which will work for them and their budget. Either way, we can help you get what you need. We've got the good stuff.

So, newsletters. For now, the novelty lies in print and mail. That doesn't mean you don't need digital formats, too, because you do. It just means that if you really want maximum impact, you'll spring for some paper, ink, and postage.

Semantics First: What Are Newsletters?

Printed or digital, a newsletter gives valuable information and news to groups of people with a common interest on a regularly (usually monthly) basis. Newsletters can come from all types of businesses and organizations – from big and small companies, local charities, and national associations. Some are paid subscriptions; some are free. The terms 'newsletters' and 'ezines' are largely interchangeable, except that newsletters can be in digital or print format while ezines are exclusively distributed online. Usually, we're looking at between 2-5 articles, and anywhere from 2-12 pages. But it's not just words. For print newsletters, if you include attractive graphics and images, your newsletter will take on the appearance of being more like a magazine, and your recipients' sense of knowing, liking, and trusting your client will skyrocket as they enjoy looking at the pictures and reading helpful, valuable, and maybe even entertaining articles. You can also include coupons and special offers that make the newsletter even more likely to be anticipated, read, and acted upon each month.

Why Do Businesses Need a Newsletter?

Businesses use newsletters to connect, teach, and sell. It's a mindshare tactic – stay on the forefront of your customers' and prospects' minds, and they're more likely to be loyal. Offer specials, be personable, and share really valuable information, and you'll cement your client's position as "my [whatever your client does]" in readers' minds.

Studies show the most common reason customers leave one business to do business with its competitor is that they felt forgotten, unappreciated, and disconnected. The name of the game is lead nurturing and customer retention – and newsletters are a cost-effective way to accomplish both.

Should you go print or digital?

Print will give you some advantages:

*   More likely to get read than digital, if the graphic design is eye-catching and the articles are engaging.
*   Not many businesses are doing print anymore, so your newsletter will stand out.

- Some people are 'over' digital overload. They're the same people who'd probably prefer holding a real book rather than a Kindle.
- You don't have to wait to build a list before you can get results for your client.

Some disadvantages:

- Print can be expensive. If your client has hundreds or thousands of people to contact, print's probably not going to happen. You'd have to be an incredible salesperson to get them to go for this.
- If they somehow DO go for this, and you don't get results from their first newsletter, you're going to be in hot water.
- If your call to action is Internet-based, readers may not take action because it's too much trouble to fire up the computer and type in the website you've asked them to visit.

Digital has its advantages:

- Deliver cost is pretty nearly zero, unless you count Aweber or whatever other email service you use. Doesn't matter whether you're sending to a handful of clients or a horde.
- Apparently every published test says sending digitally as the way to go. (Harumph.)

- If you include an Internet-related call to action, all it takes is for readers to click to follow it.

Some disadvantages:
Hello? See the poop theory above.

Do Newsletters Help with SEO?

Not especially. And especially not the ones you just print and mail. Google's good, but so far they don't have the ability to read stuff that's not online.

However, if you get unique content written for your newsletter (rather than stock content, which is an option for some businesses, and we do offer a range of packages that starts with stock content at the lower end), you can multipurpose it to use online as well as in email and print newsletters.

For example, if your newsletter is original content you can...

- Post them to your site as blog posts. This gives you more pages (hence great SEO value) to get indexed by searching and more importantly, you get ranked higher because search engines love FRESH content.

- Use them as the content of a video
- Record them and use them as audio content and podcasts
- Use them as guest posts on other website
- Allow other newsletters to use your content

Newsletters are not primarily about SEO. They're about nurturing leads, and caring for customers. The good thing about that is that it doesn't matter what Google does – the whole Google machine could go kablooey, and your newsletters will still be making money for your clients. Kind of nice to have at least one thing that's pretty nearly guaranteed to generate business, regardless of Pandas, Penguins, or whatever zoo animal Google wants to unleash next.

The ROI on Newsletters

The whole point of having a newsletter or ezine is to maintain regular contact with subscribers. This means publishing at least once a quarter, but more likely once or twice a month. Whether the newsletter goes out internally to a company's employees to build a sense of teamwork and keep them informed about industry news, out to consumers to provide a mix of relevant content and promotional material, or out to members of a non-profit organization to keep them informed about events, fundraising, and news, compiling this publication on a regular basis is a lot of work.

What Are They Reading in the John Now?

Newsletters are such an effective way to maintain contact with people and to boost ongoing revenue that they are well worth the investment they require. Smart business owners recognize the wisdom of outsourcing this task, and who better to help them than you, their marketing consultant?

Getting results from a newsletter requires having a list of subscribers, of course. Building that list is most easily done through your client's website. Using an email service like Aweber, MailChimp, or Constant Contact is the best way to manage the subscriber list and ensure newsletters get delivered. However, don't just stop there – you also want to get the information you need to be able to send a print newsletter.

For many businesses, this is a piece of cake. The billing office has all this information. If your client's business isn't that kind of business, you'll need to train them to start collecting mailing addresses as well as email addresses.

Worth the hassle? Yes! A single newsletter can easily get the phone ringing and the door swinging with customers who've been meaning to come in for a while, and just remembered when they got that newsletter. In fact, newsletters are so powerful that you can lead with them in prospecting. The speed with which they can generate business leaves SEO sitting in the dust.

Your newsletter clients will get the best results possible by planning ahead. If you will spend a bit of time planning the contents of 6-12 months of newsletters with your client, you will help them focus on their marketing thrusts for that time period as well. For many business owners, marketing is just something that happens haphazardly rather than in an organized, strategic way. By looking at what's already on the calendar for the coming months and seeing how it can be tied into the newsletter, you can also suggest ways your client can leverage these events into marketing and publicity.

If you want to market newsletter services, you might want to consider doing one for your own business. If you create a newsletter with really valuable content, teaching your subscribers how to use newsletters to grow their business, you will quickly gain expert status and find they want to hire you to publish for them, too.

How to Re-Sell Newsletter Services to Clients

1. Every business needs a newsletter. Every newsletter should be prepared for print and online use. Here's how you recognize a good prospect for this service:

- When you find business owners with a high proportion of inactive customers.

- When you find business owners who have collected the mailing addresses and/or email addresses of their customers.
- When you find business owners who are in a highly competitive niche where customers frequently change to other providers.
- When you find business owners whose products or services are especially visually appealing.
- I don't know of a business that wouldn't benefit from newsletters… except maybe a Persian rug dealer who's going out of business!

2. Ask probing questions to assess their need, and help them to see it, too:

- How often do you send out a newsletter?
- How do you stay in contact with your customers and get them to remember YOU are their [whatever their business is]?
- Do you have a mailing list? Is it email addresses, mailing addresses, or both?
- If you're sending an email newsletter only, how big is the decline you're seeing in your open rate?
- How often could you run a special that might get existing customers to come back in quickly to do more business with you?
- What would happen if even ten percent of your current customer base came in or called for an

appointment (whichever is applicable) in the next two weeks?

3. Use a checklist to analyze their newsletter plan and history:

   - Newsletters published a minimum of once per month – sent by email or in print?

   - Does each newsletter include a coupon or other special offer?

   - Are the articles written in an engaging style, and do they finish with a powerful call to action that spells out the next steps a reader should take?

   - Who has been in charge of creating the newsletters your client has sent out in the past? How much time and hassle was involved? How effective were the newsletters in generating revenue?

4. Communicate the benefits of professionally written and designed newsletters. Regular mailing can help them make more money by:

   - Keeping their business at the forefront of customers' minds, so they don't 'accidentally' forget who they usually go to for whatever products or services your client sells.

- Drumming up repeat business from customers who keep meaning to come back for more, and just needed a nudge.

- Getting readers to come in to take advantage of the coupon – and of course, they spend more while they're there.

- Positioning your client as an expert.

- Offering valuable information, then subtly compelling readers to take action.

- Building credibility – the perception is that only 'real' and successful businesses would send a newsletter.

- Potential for reusing the content to publish online, or possibly even in a book someday.

5. Present a selection of done-for-you newsletter packages.

  - Create your own newsletter packages by adding a margin to the packages of an outsource team.

  - Give each package a name. You will find that if you offer three package levels, most clients will choose the middle package.

  - For newsletter packages, you could make the frequency of publishing, the page count, the customization of the content, or the source of the info (is an interview involved?) the distinguishing mark between pricing levels.

- Add this service into your marketing materials.
- Add done-for-you newsletters to the list of services on your own website.

6. Order newsletter creation services for your client. Simply go to www.TriumphCom.com/nitro to order.

- Choose your package.
- Pay via PayPal.
- We will contact you to confirm receipt of your order and send you a questionnaire to complete on behalf of your client.
- If you prefer, for an additional fee, we can interview you or your client to extract that information (painless, we promise!) without you having to complete the questionnaire.
- We can even create an editorial calendar for orders of six or more newsletters for your approval.
- We can also interview someone from your client's office to create a custom article that sounds like them.
- We'll draft the text and graphics based on what you've approved, and send to you for final approval within a week or less, in most cases.
- If revisions are needed, just let us know, and we'll get them done and back to you quickly.

- The files for graphic-laden newsletters are usually very large. We recommend delivery to you via Dropbox.
- The ink requirements for print newsletters can be ridiculous. We recommend getting the print version produced by a commercial printer.

Sample Text for Your Website

Promote, Educate, Inform: Newsletters Make Business Easy

Newsletters are a great way to build your business. In fact, newsletters are in the top three most used business marketing tactics, according to a recent survey by MarketingProfs and Content Marketing Institute.

- Build a strong base of loyal customers
- Stay at the forefront of your customer's minds
- Promote new products, services, and special offers
- Gain credibility as an industry expert
- and more

Of course, if your subscribers don't open and read your newsletter, nothing happens. That's why now, more than ever, newsletters may be a business' best option for getting customers to come back for more.

Whether you want to publish and mail your newsletter or send out a digital version, success begins with high-quality, engaging writing.

To find out how you can use newsletters to boost your revenue, call or click today.

Newsletters may be your foot in the door to helping businesses grow. A gateway service, if you want to call it that – your clients will start with just a taste, see how much revenue each newsletter generates, then start relying on you to provide other services to them. In a world filled with SEO guys hanging from the rafters and spamming the living daylights out of business owners (seriously, you should look in your own spam folder in your email program and see how many SEO firms are hitting YOU up!), you can stand out from the crowd by offering something that really works – no matter what Google does.

Get your newsletter publishing empire started today at www.TriumphCom.com/nitro.

Ethical Bribe

*Using Ebooks
to Build Your List*

By Susan Anderson

Choice Words

Ethical Bribe:
Using Ebooks to Build Your List

Used to think that it was so easy
Used to say that it was so easy
But you're trying, you're trying now

Gerry Rafferty, Baker Street
(Oh, just YouTube it!)

Once upon a time, in the early days of the digital frontier, our forebears had only to step outside their hermit huts, ask passerby for their names and email addresses, and voila! They built big, beautiful, lists flowing with the milk and honey commonly referred to as "push-button income".

Now, getting someone's contact info looks more like the Seinfeld episode where Jerry mugs Mrs. Choate for a loaf of marble rye. (Again, YouTube is there for a reason.)

The novelty of getting email is gone, a distant memory for most people. Now, you'd better have a darned good reason for me to give you my contact info and grant access to my inbox.

Enter the ethical bribe.

A free giveaway, a gift, a free bonus, a client attraction device, or incentive – whatever you call it, this is an irresistible freebie that gets the ball rolling. It's a civilized first step in the relationship – rather than the caveman-dragging-you-by-the-hair too-much-too-soon plan of launching right into selling, like some marketers do.

Ebooks hold an appeal for prospects in that they can download them, read them when they're ready, and not be bothered with actual human interaction (like if they contacted a business offline) until they're ready to. The idea is that a business would pour all the valuable information a customer might need into their ebook – whether it's about choosing, using, or keeping up with a product or service that interests them.

That appeal is still strong enough that by using ebooks, you can ethically bribe prospects to surrender their information via opt-in box. They understand you'll be in touch after the download, and for now, they're okay with that.

Semantics First: What Is an Ebook?

This bit of content is a hot mess semantics-wise. Are we talking a special report? A Kindle book? A PDF? Is it five pages? Five hundred? Is it free? Or, do readers have to buy it?

Yes.

Let's just describe it like this – and then call it an ebook: This is a substantial piece of content that provides valuable information to readers, ultimately giving them enough education about a product, service, or topic, to get them to take the next step the publisher wishes them to take.

You might think of it in terms of shock and awe. If you were doing an ebook about local online marketing (ahem... a distinct possibility), you'd want to go into what it is, why a business needs it, what would happen if they don't have it, what's involved, all the pieces and parts that go into a local online marketing campaign, and possibly even how to do it. The goal of that information dump is to educate prospects about something they've started suspecting they need, then overwhelming them with the truth of what's involved in doing it themselves, all so their next question to you is: "Could I just pay you to do this for me?"

Why Do Businesses Need an Ebook?
Ever cooked a roast in a crock pot? You throw a bunch of stuff into this mechanical kitchen magician, put the lid on, turn it on, then go away. Several hours you've got this incredible meal, plus leftovers. You've got sandwiches, stew, hash... even a smoothie if you want to be gross.

OK, that's really gross, actually. Sorry. Think happy Nutella thoughts to cleanse the palate for a moment.

Analogy failed, but the point remains. Sometimes you can start with one thing, then slice and dice, reuse and reformat to make a whole bunch of new things.

That's how it is with an ebook. From an ebook, you could make articles, blog posts, videos, an autoresponder series, an online course, a PowerPoint presentation, a video sales letter, a speech, a webinar... you get the idea.

You could also...

- Use the ebook as an incentive to get web visitors to opt into your list
- Give away to customers as training manuals
- Sell to prospects as a way to start them spending money with the company
- Use as a lead generator... people finding out about the company through the book
- Builds the credibility of the business or spokesperson or owner, since they (almost) literally "wrote the book" on their business
- Print it out and use it at trade shows to get visitors' business cards
- Generate visibility

- Give away as bonuses to other related firm's promotions
- Attract clients (there's a true story in the industry about a CPA firm that invested in having an ebook written – it paid off in landing $5 million in fees!)
- Publish it as a buyer's guide describing to prospective customers what they should look for when buying a _____

Do Ebooks Help with SEO?

Not particularly, at least in their traditional PDF format. But that's not the point.

Actually, in some of its potential incarnations, an ebook can do great things for SEO – but you'd have to slice and dice a bit to make that happen. You could take segments and post on your client's blog or as articles backlinked to your client's site.

The thing is, not everything you do as a local online marketer is about SEO. There's more to life than SEO, man!! Get ahold of yourself!

The biggest benefit from ebooks is that they build credibility while moving prospects closer to the point of sale by providing the information they need to make a buying decision.

The ROI on Ebooks

While your clients may have some ideas for how they'd use ebooks in their business, you can add even more value by making suggestions for other marketing uses. The more value you add to their business, the more valuable you become to them as a marketing partner, and the more you can charge for your services.

Here are some examples:

- A high end real estate broker used an ebook as a bribe to get leads online for those wanting to buy or sell in this ritzy resort. He increased his leads by 20 fold and hired two people just to manage the leads…sales went through the roof!
- Many website owners see the number of people who opt into their list go from less than 5% of the visitors opting in to over 30%. The trick is in both the title and the content…a great title with bad content will backfire and great content with a lousy title won't get the job done.

Suggest that your clients use ebooks to:
- Give away at tradeshow booths

- Give away any time they give a speech or presentation
- Send it as a viral message to their existing customers and recommend they pass it along to their contacts who'd benefit from the information
- Embed links in the ebook to drive readers to their website

How to Re-Sell Ebook Services to Clients

1. Every business needs an ebook. Here's how you recognize a good prospect for this service:
   - When you find business owners who have an interesting product or service, or one that prospects might have questions about before buying.
   - When you find business owners who aren't building an email list.
   - When you find prospects who'd benefit from being positioned as an expert in their niche.
   - When you find business owners who spend a lot of time teaching their customers how to choose, use, or keep up with the products and services they sell.
   - When you find business owners who are especially passionate about their industry.

2. Ask probing questions to assess their need, and help them to see it, too:

    - Do you often get the same questions over and over from prospects?

    - Do prospects need a lot of information before they can make a buying decision?

    - How do you convey your position as an expert in your industry to people who might want to be your customer?

    - Do you have something you can give prospects that's valuable to them, but that costs you nothing beyond its initial investment to give them?

    - Do you have a way of persuading website visitors to give you their contact information and permission to email them with offers and promotions?

    - What printed or digital content do you already have that could form the basis of an ebook for your business?

3. Use a checklist to analyze their need for an ebook with them:

    - Is there an ebook that was custom-created for the business? (As opposed to an industry standard or PLR-type content)

    - If they have an ebook, is it well-written and engaging?

- How's the title? Does it make you want to drop everything and read more?

- How about the actual content? Does it make the idea of doing business with your client practically irresistible?

- Whatever they're using for an ethical bribe – is it getting good results for them?

- What's the conversion rate for how many new website visitors opt in versus how many just leave? You want to run at least 30%-50% on conversions of targeted traffic.

4. Communicate the benefits of professionally written ebooks. Publishing a custom-created ebook can help them make more money by:

    - Increasing the conversion rate of new website visitors.

    - Potentially getting some attention from local media.

    - Positioning them as experts in their fields.

    - Subtly compelling readers to take action.

    - Building credibility – the perception is that only 'real' businesses have a book.

    - Shortening the sales cycle as visitors self-serve the information they need to make a buying decision.

5. Present a selection of done-for-you ebook packages.

- Create your own ebook packages by adding a margin to the packages of an outsource team.

- Give each package a name. You will find that if you offer three package levels, most clients will choose the middle package.

- For ebook packages, you could make the length of the text, the possibility of publishing on Amazon and Kindle, or the source of the info (is an interview involved?) the distinguishing mark between pricing levels.

- Add this service into your marketing materials.

- Add done-for-you ebooks to the list of services on your own website.

6. Order ebook creation services for your client. Simply go to www.TriumphCom.com/nitro to order.

- Choose your package.

- Pay via PayPal.

- We will contact you to confirm receipt of your order and send you a questionnaire to complete on behalf of your client.

- If you prefer, for an additional fee, we can interview you or your client to extract that information (painless, we promise!) without you having to complete the questionnaire.

- We will create an outline for the ebook based on information you and your client provide along with our research of frequently asked questions for that type of business.
- We'll draft the text based on what you've approved, and send to you for final approval within two weeks or less, in most cases.
- If revisions are needed, just let us know, and we'll get them done and back to you quickly.
- We can handle getting the book into print as well, for an additional fee.

Sample Text for Your Website

Have a Great Product, Service, or Idea?
Ebooks Make It Easy to Become an Industry Leader

People love to do business with the thought leader of an industry. Creating a downloadable ebook is one of the fastest, easiest ways to become known as an authority in your field. With no printing or shipping costs, more successful business owners just like you are using ebooks:

- To establish credibility as the expert who "wrote the book" on your business

- To print and use as marketing tools to give away at trade shows, networking events, and speaking engagements
- As a great incentive for your web visitors to opt into your mailing list
- To build customer loyalty
- To provide the information prospects need as they make a buying decision
- And hundreds of other uses

Internet marketers, large corporations, and small business owners can use ebooks to generate more website traffic, leads, and sales while adding instant credibility to your business.

To learn more about how you can use ebooks to give your business a competitive edge, click or call today.

You need some way of persuading prospects to allow you to market to drip market on them, and ebooks are a credibility-building, sales curve-shortening way to give them something valuable enough for them to give you their contact information. Just like keeping certain staples in your fridge and on your shelves, an ebook gives you a starting point for content marketing.

Slice, dice, and you'll find you've got all kinds of carrots to entice prospects to come a little closer.

DRIP
email marketing nurtures leads

By Susan Anderson

Choice Words

Drip:
Email Marketing Nurtures Leads

"Don't you know? The fortune's in the follow-up," says the annoyingly ageless former beauty pageant contestant turned self-appointed business networking guru orating at a rubber chicken luncheon years ago.

Instantly, I turn into Samuel L. Jackson in Pulp Fiction. "Say, 'The fortune's in the follow-up,' ONE. MORE. TIME."

As a freelance writer and on-again, off-again hermit (a description that is NOT, in fact, redundant, thank you!), the last thing on earth I wanted to do was pester people in the name of follow up. In fact, the philosophy I practice is more Mel Brooks' "Or you got it or you ain't" when it comes to selling my services. Long ago and far away, there was time and energy for explaining to prospects why they needed professional writing. Back then, part of the persuasion piece included nudging them toward considering getting a website for their business... because it sure looked like maybe this Internet thing was more than a fad.

Prospects either get it, or they don't. I hate making follow-up calls. The thought of having to check back with people

97

to nurture them along through the sales cycle makes me want to vomit. As a Quick Start (see the Kolbe Assessment if you haven't already), I may lack the genetic material that makes patient lead nurturing possible. As a creative, the idea of making sales calls is about as repulsive as it gets.

Good thing there are ways to work around that. Automated, yet personalized ways. Ways you can set and forget, and not have to worry about having forgotten to reach out.

And, even if you LOVE following up with leads, maybe your clients don't.

Let's talk about email marketing, an easy, automated way you can lead those horses to water and get them drinking.

Semantics First: What Is Email Marketing?

Email marketing is a form of permission marketing. By subscribing to a business' email list, usually in exchange for being able to download a free ebook or report, customers and prospects give permission to be contacted on a regular basis to get information and offers that may be valuable to them. It's an excellent example of drip marketing, where rather than flooding prospects with a fire hose volume of information all at once, you lead them step by step into your sales funnel.

There are two sorts of messages involved in email marketing: autoresponders and broadcast messages. An autoresponder is a series of emails that are queued and ready to be sent at certain intervals when a customer subscribes to a business' email list. They go out in a set sequence no matter when the subscription starts. Broadcast messages are sent at will, whenever you've got a newsletter, special promotion, blog post you want to blast out, or some other time-sensitive message to get out. Together, autoresponders and broadcast messages form a follow-up marketing funnel that is very inexpensive, and if done well, effective.

Why Do Businesses Need Email Marketing?

Email marketing is one of the cheapest ways any business can create a steady flow of revenue – either from online or in-office sales. With no printing costs and no postage, it's easy to stay in regular contact with customers and prospects. Most marketing wisdom says you need to "touch" your customers about thirteen times a year in order to stay in the forefront of their minds. There's no easier way to do this, or to automate this process, than by using email marketing and autoresponders.

Generally, a website visitor subscribes in order to get a free report or other giveaway, then confirms that subscription and becomes eligible to receive emails from the business.

Highly automated online businesses may have hundreds of emails queued in their autoresponder service, going out to subscribers at prescribed intervals. This makes it possible to create a steady flow of sales as new subscribers enter the funnel all the time.

Many business owners have heard they should be using email marketing, but have yet to implement what they have learned. Others have email marketing campaigns in place that are less than effective because they are not well written, or they have so few messages in their autoresponders that they are missing out on sales.

Small business owners are also beginning to use email marketing more often now. It's not uncommon to find an email sign-up sheet on the counter of a salon, dentist's office, or even some restaurants. Nearly every time you complete an intake form to receive service at a local business, there's a line for your email address.

The problem is that many of these businesses are collecting email addresses from all their customers without knowing what to do with them – or how to do it without violating spam rules. Some may even be trying to send mass emails using their own private email address. If you can present the benefits of using an email and autoresponder marketing strategy, suggest resources to do it right, and provide professional writing services they can use, they will be happy to hand this task over to you rather than trying to do it themselves.

Does Email Marketing Help with SEO?

Not directly, because the search engines aren't scanning your email messages for ranking purposes. However, if you've got unique content, you can slice and dice it to make for some nice blog posts.

While it may not be all that effective for SEO, here are some interesting statistics from HubSpot about the current state of email marketing:

- 80.8% of users report reading email on mobile devices (HubSpot)
- 12% of people use separate work and personal inboxes (HubSpot)
- Over 50% of respondents say they read most of their emails (HubSpot)
- Secrets is the most clicked lead nurturing subject line word (HubSpot)
- Posts and Jobs are the most clicked subject line words (HubSpot)

- Click through rate (CTR) is higher when using the recipient's first name in the subject line over no use of the first name (HubSpot)
- CTR is higher when using the recipient's company name in the subject line over no company mention (HubSpot)
- 88% prefer to receive HTML emails vs. 12% who prefer plain text from companies (HubSpot)
- 65% prefer emails that contain mostly images vs. 35% who prefer mostly text (HubSpot)
- Your most recent subscribers are the most likely to click through (HubSpot)
- Saturday has the highest CTR at over 9% (Sunday is second just under 9%) (HubSpot)
- 6 AM has the highest CTR of any hour (HubSpot)
- Most unsubscriptions come on Tuesdays (0.52% unsub rate) (HubSpot)
- Clicks by button text: Click Here gets the highest % of clicks over Go and Submit (HubSpot)

The ROI on Email Marketing

Email marketing can be one of the most profitable marketing tactics any business can use – or it can be a complete waste of time; it all depends on whether it's done correctly. Because practically anyone can send an email, some business owners may initially think they don't need professional help to do this. However, providing a quick rundown of the benefits of doing email marketing well and the hazards of doing it incorrectly is often enough to persuade prospective clients of the value of outsourcing this task.

The biggest benefit of email marketing is that it is an automated yet customized way a business can "touch" customers and prospects and drive sales. Because most business owners are extremely busy working in and on their businesses, handling every aspect from bookkeeping to customer service, being able to outsource a task like this – and have it create revenue – is an easy decision.

Good blog posts paired with an autoresponder sequence can feed off of one another to get double duty from both. Any time you write a blog post that draws a lot of comments, website traffic, and sales for your client, see how you could repurpose that content as an autoresponder message to add to the queue. Likewise, if you have an email message that is especially effective, consider how you could repurpose and reword it to include on the blog. Don't worry about repeating the same core message in different media. Every business has its own set of stories that will appear over and over as part of the branding and core message.

An effective email marketing campaign accomplishes three major goals. It can:

- Deliver content that boosts your client's credibility with subscribers.
- Get sales.
- Get subscribers to take action, whether it's to buy something, provide a testimonial, comment on a blog, or anything else.

There are two major types of emails you can create for a client – broadcasts and autoresponders. A broadcast goes out immediately to your client's entire list at the same time. Autoresponders are a pre-programmed series of emails that go out at set intervals. Broadcast emails that are especially effective should be added to the autoresponder series to help automate the marketing process.

Do NOT allow your clients to send email marketing messages through their personal or business email accounts. Internet service providers are vigilant in monitoring email volume to counteract SPAM and have been known to ban people for sending out mass emails. There are a number of email services your clients can use to safely send thousands of emails. For a very small monthly fee, these services will maintain the subscriber list (handling unsubscribes, bounces, etc.), give the emails the best possible chance for delivery, allow for scheduled intervals for delivery, and in some cases, track the open rate for each message.

How to Re-Sell Email Marketing Services to Clients

Any local business from a hair salon to an oil change place could benefit from email marketing. The business owner could collect email addresses from customers and send out discount offers, reminders to come in for service, seasonal promotions, and information about new services and products. Emails could also include tips that will be useful to their customers.

Put together a one-page flyer that highlights the benefits and process of starting up an email and autoresponder campaign. Give this information to small business owners you meet while you're out in your everyday life as well as when you're at networking events. Remember, the more information you give away, the more likely you are to find great clients.

1. Every business needs email marketing. Every email marketing campaign needs messages. Here's how you recognize a good prospect for this service:
   - When you find business owners who have an email list they're not marketing to.
   - When you find business owners who aren't following up with prospects.

- When you find clients who have content in some form, but aren't using it in a systematized, automated way to get more business.

2. Ask probing questions to assess their need, and help them to see it, too:

   - How often do you send out email marketing messages?

   - How many autoresponder messages do you have in your queue?

   - What email service are you using in your email marketing campaign?

   - What's your open rate? Click through rate? Unsubscribe rate?

   - Who writes autoresponders and broadcast messages for you?

   - What happens after someone downloads your ebook?

   - How many contacts do you find it takes before a prospect becomes a customer, and how do you make sure they get that many 'touches'?

3. Use a checklist to analyze their current email marketing plan and message content with them:

- A series of autoresponders is attached to their site so that people who opt in start getting messages automatically.

- Broadcast messages are sent a minimum of once per month.

- Does each email message in the queue have an engaging headline that makes you want to click and read?

- Each email message includes a powerful call to action that spells out the next steps a reader should take.

4. Communicate the benefits of professionally written email marketing messages. Autoresponders and broadcasts can help them make more money by:

- Dripping your marketing message onto your prospects, nurturing the leads you attract through other marketing methods.

- Decreasing the hands-on work of prospect follow-up.

- Subtly compelling readers to take action.

- Building credibility – the perception is that only 'real' businesses send email messages.

- Keeping a business at the forefront of prospects' and customers' minds so they are more likely to do business with you rather than your competitor.

5. Present a selection of done-for-you email marketing packages.

   - Create your own email marketing message packages by adding a margin to the packages of an outsource team.

   - Give each package a name. You will find that if you offer three package levels, most clients will choose the middle package.

   - For email marketing packages, you could make the quantity of messages, creation of an editorial calendar, the source of the info (is an interview involved?), or done-for-you loading into an email marketing service the distinguishing mark between pricing levels.

   - Add this service into your marketing materials.

   - Add done-for-you email marketing to the list of services on your own website.

6. Order email marketing message creation services for your client. Simply go to www.TriumphCom.com/nitro to order.

   - Choose your package.

   - Pay via PayPal.

   - We will contact you to confirm receipt of your order and send you a questionnaire to complete on behalf of your client.

- If you prefer, for an additional fee, we can interview you or your client to extract that information (painless, we promise!) without you having to complete the questionnaire.

- We'll draft the text based on what you've approved, and send to you for final approval within a week or less, in most cases.

- If revisions are needed, just let us know, and we'll get them done and back to you quickly.

- We can handle uploading to your client's email provider, or even post to your client's website as blog posts for you, for an additional fee.

- We can even create an ebook for your client if they don't have one already. This makes for an excellent ethical bribe to get prospects to opt in.

Sample Text for Your Website

What If You Could "Set It and Forget It" with Email Marketing?
Autoresponders Make Marketing Easy

They say "the fortune's in the follow-up" – and that's never more accurate than when it comes to staying in touch with prospects and customers who visit your website.

Because it can take several exposures to your offer before a prospect makes a buying decision, you've got two choices:

Spend your time following up with prospects, making as many as 12 different contacts before you see results.

OR

Let a series of customized emails do it for you, automatically.

Email marketing is a super-efficient way you can answer your prospects' unspoken objections, show them the benefits of using your products and services, build your credibility and position yourself as an expert with the answers and information they need, and... close more sales.

Call or click today to find out how email marketing can drive sales to your business.

So, whether you loooove making follow-up calls or would rather walk barefoot over a lego-covered floor in the dark, you can use email marketing to make follow-up more effective. It's an easy way to automate some of the marketing for any business. Statistics show people who don't buy on the first introduction to an offer take several more "touches" before they decide to buy. By having those touches automated, they're more likely to happen than if a business owner has to remember to follow up manually.

LINKS
JUST GOT
REAL

RIP
Article
Marketing

Why Businesses STILL Need Articles

By Susan Anderson

Choice Words

Links Just Got Real:
Why Businesses STILL Need Articles

"It was the best of times, it was the worst of times,
it was the age of wisdom, it was the age of foolishness,
it was the epoch of belief, it was the epoch of incredulity,
it was the season of Light, it was the season of Darkness,
it was the spring of hope, it was the winter of despair,
we had everything before us, we had nothing before us,
we were all going direct to Heaven,
we were all going direct the other way…"

Charles Dickens, A Tale of Two Cities

Chuck could just have easily been writing about the page rank slaughter that we now refer to as Google's Penguin Update. Maybe even the Panda.

How many SEO firms bit the dust during this bleak episode in our industry's history? Even those that played by the rules still bear bloody beak marks on their rumps, evidence that the Big G will not be trifled with.

Spinners? Like playing with dynamite.

Submission bots? Russian roulette.

Gone are the days of cranking out articles like Pez, slinging them around online all willy-nilly just to get backlinks.

Freelance writers did not escape the fiery breath of the Penguin, either. At one point, my business had a client who ordered over a thousand articles on custom t-shirts (you know, like Café Press... but not them). We wrote until our imaginations were exhausted, our fingertips ached, and our Paypal accounts filled up. He spun, posted, and ordered more.

Then all of a sudden... gone. No more article marketing orders. The very writing project I'd built a full-time income on, the one Eben Pagan featured me on for his "Get Ignition" course... just gone. Nobody wanted to touch articles.

It wasn't articles that was the problem; it was how they were getting used and abused. Marketers were spinning them into oblivion, then posting in thousands of article directories, where they'd get scraped and re-published into thousands of other article directories. The problem was, these spun articles sucked. (Sorry, Mom, I know you don't like that word, but it fits.) The original articles probably weren't much to look at, but after a couple dozen rounds in a spinner, they were just hideous.

And we wondered why Google's Penguin came out swinging.

The whole point of Google is delivering relevant, valuable content (ultimately, so it can make gazillions of dollars). If marketers polluted the articlesphere with this kind of garbage, and Google didn't slap them silly, they'd lose market share.

Article directories went bye-bye. They got smacked hard for having non-existent standards for submissions. Even the good directories got hit.

So what's left for article marketing? Is it worthwhile?

Yes, but you'll have to forget everything you thought you knew about it.

Semantics First: What Is Article Marketing (Now)?

Used to be that article marketing meant creating a 500-ish word article and submitting it to article sites like EzineArticles.com. Getting a little fancier, maybe you'd spin them and submit through an automated submission service. The result then would be thousands of backlinks pointing at your site. Cool, in practice… crappy in reality. Spun content is almost always the Internet equivalent of playing "telephone", except with cavemen. The flow, the style, the context all take a hit.

Now that Google smacked that tactic into oblivion, it's all about high quality versus quantity.

Article marketing now covers a spectrum, starting with writing articles and manually submitting them to just a few sites, like EzineArticles, up to writing what would be considered link bait or feature articles – extremely high quality, like that might go into a trade journal or that could be considered a masterpiece for the author.

Pricing used to resemble buying stuff in bulk. There were article writers out there cranking out one-pagers for $5. (Not me, ahem.) Remember, the name of the game was quantity, and it was all going to get spun anyhow.

Articles range from just a few hundred words to a few thousand, but the most common type are in the 500-word range. They are written from all kinds of angles, from straight-forward news to product reviews, how-to's to personal accounts.

The best way to approach article marketing now is to forget that old way ever existed. Now, think of it as a mini report, something a subject matter expert would write and be proud to publish.

You can slice and dice these subject matter expert articles and use them on blogs, in newsletters, as the basis for a video, and more – but let's just not confuse the semantics of "article marketing" because the old way will just get you in trouble.

There are dozens of types of articles you could provide for your clients. Here is a sampling:

- academic articles
- blog posts
- articles for wikis and encyclopedias
- marketing articles
- weekly or daily columns
- essays
- how-to articles
- human interest stories
- interviews
- newsletter content
- op-ed pieces
- personal experience
- personality profiles
- service articles
- sidebars for newsletters and periodicals

- travel articles
- tips articles
- product reviews
- list articles (top 10, etc.)
- investigative articles

Why Do Businesses Need Articles?

Now that you're no longer thinking "spin and blast" when you think of article marketing, let's look at how a business can profit from publishing articles.

Business owners use articles for SEO purposes, to position themselves as experts, to get website traffic, to retain customer loyalty, in traditional print media, and much more. While most traditional print publications now have online versions, there's still the possibility of getting your client's article into print. I won't lie and tell you it's easy or that it's a sure thing, because the process is filled with uncertainty and rejection. It involved submitting queries to publishers, proposing to write an article they'll consider for some long-distant future edition of their publication. Most queries are ignored or politely declined, and it's easy to compile a stack of rejection letters deep enough to cure you of the idea that you'll ever get your client's name in print.

However, if you broaden your idea of article marketing to include guest blogging, writing articles for niche web publications, and for newsletters or trade journals, it's another story entirely. Every single website owner needs articles. Many of them recognize this need and are actively looking for great content.

Even though anyone anywhere can get published articles published online, high-quality articles are a sure way to build a perception of expertise. Imagine if you go looking online for information on a topic and you find several useful, credible articles on someone's website. It'll begin to look like this website is the absolute authority on that topic. You'll appreciate the information you get, begin to trust the site owner, and be open to hearing any other information you can get there.

Enterprise relies on an exchange of value. Smart businesses give value first before asking consumers to part with their cash. They understand the value of creating a crowd of loyal customers who wouldn't dream of going elsewhere with their business. Nowhere but the Internet has this been so easy to do.

When people have a question, a need, or a problem, they go online to find answers and solutions. Sometimes these are very personal, pressing, painful issues – other times, the searcher is a lot more casual. Either way, when they go searching, it's with a pretty high level of skepticism. They're hoping they'll find good information, but halfway expecting they'll end up sorting through a bunch of ads, taking their chances on a solution that might turn out to be the online equivalent of snake oil.

If they stumble onto articles that meet them where they are, provide good information, and lead them to a solution that looks realistically promising, there's a virtual relationship created that's going to benefit everyone involved.

Do Articles Help with SEO?

The most effective way to train the search engines to associate any website with any specific topic is to position the site as an authority on that topic. That's done by creating and publishing high-quality, relevant content – articles!

With Google's newly enforced emphasis on quality, there are also a couple of ways they reward authors of excellent articles. Author Markup and Google Authorship are still evolving, but should yield powerful SEO results when used correctly with really good articles.

One of the most powerful SEO-boosting bits isn't even in the article itself. It's the About the Author blurb that comes afterward. You wouldn't believe how often authors waste that precious real estate. In this little bit of text, you can link (depending on editorial guidelines, often TWICE!) to your website using your anchor text. The reprint rules for article directories require publishers to leave the About box text untouched. The better the article, the more it gets read and republished, and the more high-quality backlinks you get.

The ROI on Article Marketing
Articles can be repurposed to create videos and audios. Both of these are valuable assets to any business because they help create a perception of expertise, are highly favored by search engines, and are some of the most frequently forwarded kind of content out there. By turning an article into a video or audio, it can take on a whole new life.

Some other ways to repurpose articles:
- content for your newsletters
- content for other people's newsletters
- modify and use as a blog post
- modify and use for public speaking engagements
- include in marketing materials
- submission to print publications
- compile to form an ebook
- convert them into other languages and distribute online
- use them in an autoresponder series
- modify and use them for a home study course

- turn them into a PowerPoint presentation
- use them to create a press release
- modify and use in an employee manual
- modify and use for an FAQ page on a website
- and many more!

How to Re-Sell Article Creation Services to Clients

1. Every business needs articles. Here's how you recognize a good prospect for this service:

    - When you find business owners who have a lot of printed materials that could be used for creating online content.

    - When you find business owners whose websites are sparse when it comes to content.

    - When you find clients who speak well, but don't have much written content.

    - When you find prospects who are experts in their niche and who would agree to be interviewed to get that information into written form.

2. Ask probing questions to assess their need, and help them to see it, too:

    - How often do you write articles and get them published either online or offline?

    - How many articles do you have that you haven't published online yet?

- Do you have any connection with the editors of trade journals or other articles that might be interested in an article written by you?
- Tell me about your content marketing plan for the coming year.
- Do you have an editorial calendar created yet?
- Have you set up your Google Author profile yet?

3. Use a checklist to analyze their current article publishing plan with them:
   - An editorial calendar showing a systematized plan for creating and publishing articles throughout the year.
   - Accounts with EzineArticles and article directories within their niche.
   - Set up for Google Authorship and Author Markup
   - Looking at previously created articles, are the headlines engaging? Is the text written at between the 5th and 8th grade level? Does each article have a call to action at the end? Is it an enjoyable read that makes you want to read more?

4. Communicate the benefits of professionally written articles. Articles can help them make more money by:

    • Dripping your marketing message onto your prospects, nurturing the leads you attract through other marketing methods.

    • Decreasing the hands-on work of prospect follow-up.

    • Subtly compelling readers to take action.

    • Building credibility – the perception is that only 'real' businesses publish articles.

    • Reaching into the audiences of other business owners who've gathered your client's ideal customers already.

5. Present a selection of done-for-you article packages.

    • Create your own article creation packages by adding a margin to the packages of an outsource team.

    • Give each package a name. You will find that if you offer three package levels, most clients will choose the middle package.

    • For article creation packages, you could make the quantity or length of articles, creation of an editorial calendar, the source of the info (is an interview involved?), or done-for-you distribution to EzineArticles.com the distinguishing mark between pricing levels.

- Add this service into your marketing materials.
- Add done-for-you article creation to the list of services on your own website.

6. Order article creation services for your client. Simply go to www.TriumphCom.com/nitro to order.

   - Choose your package.
   - Pay via PayPal.
   - We will contact you to confirm receipt of your order and send you a questionnaire to complete on behalf of your client.
   - If you prefer, for an additional fee, we can interview you or your client to extract that information (painless, we promise!) without you having to complete the questionnaire.
   - We'll draft the text based on what you've approved, and send to you for final approval within a week or less, in most cases.
   - If revisions are needed, just let us know, and we'll get them done and back to you quickly.
   - We can handle uploading to your client's EzineArticles account for no additional fee.

Sample Text for Your Website

Looking for More Website Traffic?
High-Quality Articles Generate Website Traffic, Increase Revenues

You could spend a fortune on Pay Per Click ads, and get a bunch of traffic tomorrow. Of course, when you stop paying for the ads, they go away – and so does your traffic. Plus, your site will only appear in the "sponsored ads" section – a clear signal to your prospective buyers that you had to buy your way into the top listings.

Want a better plan?

High-quality professionally written articles can help you build your online presence and credibility. With content marketing, not only will you get better traffic more cheaply, but you'll start taking over the coveted top spots among the organic listings.

Call or click today, and find out how to use high-quality articles to start a stream of traffic that won't stop.

So, even though the shooting-fish-in-a-barrel golden age of article marketing seems to be done for now, articles still form the basis of any solid content marketing strategy. The article has grown up from being sloppy and all over the place, to a much more dignified and high-quality piece that speaks on behalf of an expert.

Supremely Sticky

The Sweetness That Is Video Marketing

Susan Anderson

Choice Words

Supremely Sticky: The Sweetness That Is Video Marketing

Ain't nobody got time for that

Ain't nobody got time for that.

Ain't nobody got time, ain't nobody got time

Ain't nobody got time for that.

Well, I woke up to go get me a cold pop

Then I thought somebody was barbequing

I said, "Oh Lord Jesus, it's a fire!"

Then I ran out, I didn't grab no shoes or nothing, Jesus

I ran for my life!

Ain't nobody got time for that

Ain't nobody got time for that.

Ain't nobody got time, ain't nobody got time

Ain't nobody got time for that.

Sweet Brown

http://www.youtube.com/watch?v=Nh7UgAprdpM

Let me tell you one thing about that video. Like some alien force, it crept into my ears, slid into my brain, and took root. I could not shake it. Day and night, I kept replaying it on a loop. I hummed the tune. I shared it. I even made friendly bets with friends that if they watched it twice, it would stick in their brains as well. It would NOT go away... for a whole week.

133

My daughter got me hooked on "Your Grammar Sucks" on YouTube (http://www.youtube.com/user/jacksfilms). In it, this guy Jack reads the butchered, crazily spelled and bizarrely worded comments strewn about the Internet. He does these voices and faces that crack me up, and the way some of these comments are written, it's just amazing to hear him attempt to read them out loud.

Then, of course (since I'm revealing that I am, in fact, a 12-year-old) there is Smosh…
(http://www.youtube.com/user/smosh). Ian and Anthony produce new videos each week that are both clearly rather 'inappropriate' (guaranteeing they'll be a hit with the high school crowd) and sometimes laugh out loud funny. (Guys Guide to Hugging Guys, for example).

Oh yes. Take a moment to look these videos up on YouTube, and look at just one thing: how many views they've got.

If you're wondering whether you ought to be doing video for your clients, the answer is YES.

If you're wondering how you'll get millions of views for your videos, stop. You probably won't. Although, it could happen…

But, not the point.

The point is this: People love to watch videos. Videos can grab attention and make people keep watching.

A friend of mine was mentoring a Real Estate agent. He wanted to know how to get more leads in his particular city. He created a video describing A Visitor's Guide for his area and explained it in a video. His leads increased 2,000%. What happens over at Google HQ when someone stays on one of your client's web pages because they're watching a video for a couple of minutes?

You get a gold star. That page is considered high quality, because visitors stay there longer than usual. Google likes that kind of stuff. And guess what else? These things actually convert!

Here's just a few minutes' worth of statistics for your reading enjoyment…

- SEOMOZ concludes that posts with videos included will attract 3 times more in-linking domains than a plain text post.
- It's been shown that videos can increase the number of business profile clicks by more than 30%, business calls by 18%, website visits by 55%,

incidence of purchase by 24%, according to a report by PRWeb.

- Via the Marketing Maven Blog, 64% of industrial companies are increasing their spend on online video. 46% now have video content on their Web sites.

- As posted in a KISSmetrics blog, viewers of a product video are 64-85% more likely to buy after watching.

- REELSEO communicates that the average social video ad campaign generated a 30% increase in additional value above the media spend by being shared.

- An eMartketer article revealed that nearly 87% of U.S. brands and agencies leveraged video for their content marketing programs.

- People were over 2x more likely to visit a site upon seeing a video than control subjects who had not watched the video in a comScore study, reported wooshi.

- Invodo video stats show that video and other multi-media product viewing options were rated more effective than any other site initiatives in an Adobe survey of almost 2,000 interactive marketers.

- Dr. James McQuivey of Forrester Research says a minute of video is worth 1.8 million words, on invodo.

- SEO Hacker states there are 1.5 million business-oriented search queries in YouTube every week.

- Video appears in 70% of the top 100 search listings, explains KISSmetrics.

- Videos are 53 times more likely than text pages to show up on the first page of search results, GIGAmon describes.

- According to MediaPost, YouTube is the 2nd largest search engine after Google.

- In a Forbes study, it was found that: three-quarters (75%) of executives surveyed said they watch work-related videos on business-related websites at least weekly; more than half (52%) watch work-related videos on YouTube at least weekly.

- GIGAom estimates almost 60% of C-level and senior executives said they would watch a video before reading text on the same web page.

- Forbes indicates, 65% of senior executives have visited a vendor's website after watching a video.

- More than half of senior executives share videos with colleagues at least weekly, and receive work-related videos as often, says Forbes.

- Forbes surveys asked about their preferred length of work-related videos, nearly half (47%) the senior executives in the survey said between 3-5 minutes.

- In a Marketing Sherpa article: regularly posting videos helped the company's website receive 200% to 300% more monthly unique visitors and a 100% longer average time-on-site spent per visitor. The average time spent on pages with videos was 3 minutes compared to 1 minute and 30 seconds averaged on pages without videos.

- According to several case studies, videos on landing pages have increased conversion rates by 32%, 86%, and 130.5%, says the MarketingTech blog.

- A case study on unbounce states that Vidyard lifted conversion rates by 100% with video on landing pages in lightbox modal popup. The average conversion rate was 6.5% without video, 11% with video embedded in the page, and 13% with video in lightbox modal popup.

- Zappos saw increases of 6% to 30% in sales for their products that had a video accompaniment, explains iMPACT.

- Video's share in US Online Ad Spending is expected to be 7.9% in 2012 and 15% in 2016, says eMarketer.

- eConsultancy says: Cisco expects video to account for 57% of consumer internet traffic by 2015, nearly four times as much as regular web browsing and email.

- FOLIOmag.com says video is used by 52% of marketers doing custom content marketing.

Hey, I can go all day here, but you get the point: You'd better get cracking on using video!

Semantics First: What Is Video Marketing?

The world of online marketing is slowly changing. While the power of the written word used to reign supreme online, the advent of online video has made video marketing all the more important.

Every video needs a script. Video scripts are documents that are specifically written to be read aloud. They can be read by a presenter on camera or they can be read as a voiceover on a video presentation. Videos are used to pre-sell a market on an idea, instruct them on how to do a specific task, answer questions from the market and a variety of other purposes. Anything that can be covered in articles or blog posts can be covered in videos. Some topics, like how to topics, are enhanced by the use of video.

A video script writer creates what is said on the screen. Depending on the client's needs, you may also be suggesting what images or steps should be showed on the screen while the script is being read. For example, you may suggest that a certain type of picture be used to illustrate a point... or, as many marketers are doing now, you may go with a completely white background, black text, and slides with just a phrase-worth of text at a time.

Video scripts can be anywhere from a single paragraph to a few pages. The length of the script will depend on how much time is allowed for the video presentation. A 30 second long video will need about 90 words.

Why Do Businesses Need Video Marketing?
Video marketing is sweeping through all aspects of Internet marketing. From independent Internet marketing professionals to corporations, you can find many prospects for this service. Many local businesses are catching on to the idea that online videos are a good marketing tool. The only problem is that most of them don't realize that using the right words in video marketing is of prime importance. Those that truly want to get the most out of video marketing will seek your help make their videos the most effective they can be.

Targeting your client's customers and potential customers with videos is a smart way to market online. Videos are becoming more and more popular online every day. Videos grab attention online, and are an excellent way to win the search engines' favor. Google integrates video search results in its regular search engine results. This means that from a marketing perspective, your clients may be more likely to rank well for a keyword term with a video rather than an article or a piece of writing.

Your prospective video clients have all experienced watching TV commercials that fall flat or worse, and many have probably tried doing their own videos and seen just how badly that can go. Combined, these two experiences make the idea of writing their own video script and producing a video seem almost impossible. To avoid a cringe-worthy final result, many of these business owners would far rather team up with a professional video creator.

Does Video Marketing Help with SEO?
You bet your bippy. Did you READ those stats a few pages ago?

And if you've learned how to speed-rank videos, you could build an entire business just producing videos for clients to get them multiple front page listings.

Just as a series of articles or a sales letter could be transformed into a video with a bit of slicing and dicing, you can work the same magic on a video script in reverse. From one video script, you could create articles, blog posts, a special report, or the basis for a sales letter.

If your client is using video marketing to build backlinks and drive traffic to a website, just creating the video isn't enough. The video has to be distributed online to all the major video sharing sites in order to accomplish traffic generation and SEO goals.

The ROI on Video Marketing

There's a lot of potential for slice and dice in video marketing. Blog posts, articles, website content, ebooks, case studies, white papers… all of these pieces can be used to form the basis of a video.

But you can't just turn an article into a video. (Although I do seem to remember some sort of software a while back where you could do this and have this robotic voice read the article while the text rolled on a teleprompter. It kind of sucked.)

Unlike some other types of online writing, like articles or blog posts, video marketing scripts are highly customized to your client's needs. This isn't to say that articles and blog posts aren't customized, but since videos come in many different formats, it's important to understand how the video is going to be produced and how it is going to be used.

There are several different production methods for video marketing. Videos may be produced by having on-camera talent reading the script. The script may be read as a voice-over to a PowerPoint presentation or other on-screen animation. The script may also serve as a tutorial that will show how to accomplish something (like setting up a new blog post). Since these different uses will make a difference in how the script is written, you need to ask about the production methods before you begin writing the script.

In addition, you need to ask about where the content will be hosted. There are three basic types of videos used for marketing purposes.

Viral videos – Viral videos are designed to drive traffic back to the website. They are created to grab attention and encourage viewers to share the videos. Anything that is inspiring, controversial or just plain funny is likely to be a good viral video.

Conversion videos – Conversion videos are hosted on the company's homepage. They are created to help the company move the visitor to a specific conversion goal. For example, a company may want their visitors to opt in to their list to receive more information. The video will be designed to explain the benefits of opting into the list and an explanation of how to go about doing so. A conversion video will always have a clear call to action.

Educational videos – Educational videos are designed to help the user learn more about a specific topic. For example, a professional organizer's website can include a video on how to tackle the "junk drawer" that most houses seem to have. The purpose of educational videos is to build loyalty with a target market. A customer is more likely to remember a company or a service provider who has offered an educational video and hire them when they are ready to buy.

Before you begin the project, determine the video's purpose and where it will be displayed. Determining this first will help you help us to create the right kind of video script. There's a big difference between the script for a viral video and a script for an educational video. If the client isn't sure which they'll need, coach them on their different options and help them determine how the video will be used.

How to Re-Sell Video Creation Services to Clients

1. Every business needs video marketing. Every video needs a script. Here's how you recognize a good prospect for this service:

   - When you find business owners who don't have any videos on their site.

   - When you find business owners who have a great personality driving their customer loyalty and sales.

   - When you find clients who have content in some form, but aren't using it in a systematized, automated way to get more business.

2. Ask probing questions to assess their need, and help them to see it, too:

   - How often do you do marketing videos?

   - Do you have a YouTube channel yet?

   - Are you multi-purposing your articles, blog posts, and other written materials to make videos?

   - Are your competitors producing videos – online or on TV?

3. Use a checklist to analyze their current video marketing plan with them:

   - Do they have a branded YouTube channel?

   - Do they create at least one marketing per month?

- Is each video promoted with a press release, blog post, newsletter mention, and social media?
- Does each video include a powerful call to action that spells out the next steps a viewer should take?

4. Communicate the benefits of professionally created videos and scripts. Marketing videos can help them make more money by:

   - Dripping your marketing message onto your prospects, nurturing the leads you attract through other marketing methods.
   - Making it easy for your existing customers to spread the word about your business to their contacts.
   - Subtly compelling viewers to take action.
   - Building credibility – the perception is that only 'real' businesses create videos.
   - Frequent video creation keeps a business at the forefront of prospects' and customers' minds so they are more likely to do business with you rather than your competitor.

5. Present a selection of done-for-you video marketing packages.

   - Create your own video marketing packages by adding a margin to the packages of an outsource team.

- Give each package a name. You will find that if you offer three package levels, most clients will choose the middle package.
- For video marketing packages, you could make the quantity of videos, creation of an editorial calendar, the source of the info (is an interview involved?), the style of the video, or done-for-you promotion services the distinguishing mark between pricing levels.
- Add this service into your marketing materials.
- Add done-for-you video marketing to the list of services on your own website.

6. Order video creation services for your client. Simply go to www.TriumphCom.com/nitro to order.

- Choose your package.
- Pay via PayPal.
- We will contact you to confirm receipt of your order and send you a questionnaire to complete on behalf of your client.
- If you prefer, for an additional fee, we can interview you or your client to extract that information (painless, we promise!) without you having to complete the questionnaire.

- We'll draft the text and slides based on what you've approved, and send to you for final approval within a week or less, in most cases.
- If revisions are needed, just let us know, and we'll get them done and back to you quickly.
- We can handle scripts, slides, voiceovers, video creation, uploading to your client's YouTube account, or even post to your client's website for you, for an additional fee.

Sample Text for Your Website

You've Got a Story to Tell – Video Tells It Best

For marketing, educating, inspiring, or taking your business viral, you can't beat the power of video. On the increasingly visual medium of the Internet, nothing speaks louder than video.

But if you've ever seen a TV commercial that fell flat, you know this is not a tactic without risk. Skimp on your marketing video, and you'll be lucky if nobody sees it. Work with a professional video scriptwriter to make sure your message reaches its target audience and gets the results you want.

Take the first step in creating a video that captivates your market, shoots you to the top of the search engine results, becomes the next viral mega-hit on YouTube, or sells your product like never before.

Call or click for your free video marketing consultation.

Are you going to create the next megahit, multi-million views video for your client? Who knows… but if you do, and if it's totally hypnotically addicting to the point viewers are watching it over and over, PLEASE do not share it with me.

'Cuz… ain't nobody got time for that!

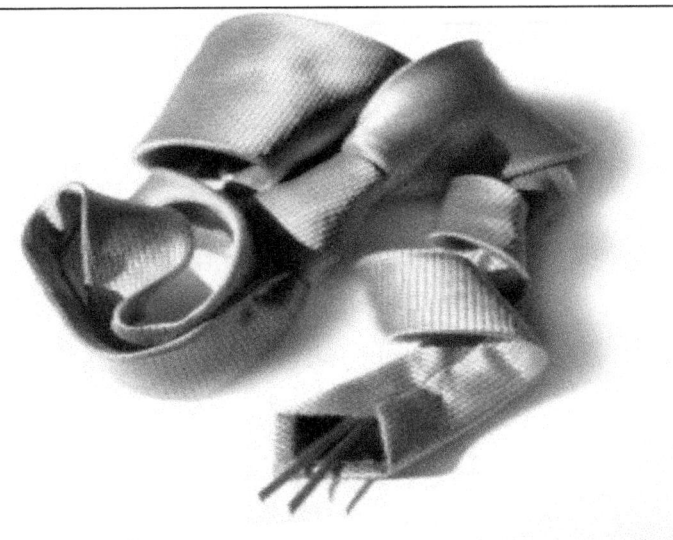

KILL THE SLEAZE

Case Studies Beat Slick Sales Guys with a Stick

BY SUSAN ANDERSON

Choice Words

Kill the Sleaze: Case Studies Beat Slick Sales Guys with a Stick

Imagine you're shopping for a new dishwasher. You're wandering through the appliance section of the home improvement store, eager to bag this purchase and be done with it. All the models start to look the same.

Then you feel it. That little hitch in your heart rate that can only come from the realization that you have become prey. You spot him angling his way toward you. Cheesy tie, scuffed shoes squeaking on the linoleum, and…. wait for it… HOHHHHH… he exhales and sniffs to be sure the scent of his bologna and onion sammich isn't going to send you running. The salesman enters.

All you really want to do is make a decision you won't regret within a year or two, get a dishwasher, and get out of there.

Then it happens.

Some other shopper walks up to you and says, "Hey, if you're thinking of buying that dishwasher right there, you should do it. I'd gotten a really bad dishwasher before that, a total waste of money. But I bought that same model you're looking at a year ago and love it. No more scraping dried bits of food off of my plates. It's a quiet machine. It's never given me a hassle of any kind. I'd buy it again without hesitation."

Sold.

That is the power of a good testimonial. It's also what lies at the core of a case study. If you learn how to produce powerful case studies for your own business and your clients, and you'll see the results in the revenue numbers.

Semantics First: What Are Case Studies?

A case study is sort of like a testimonial on steroids. It's a bit like a special report dedicated solely to how a product or service made a significant, measurable difference for a specific person facing a substantial challenge. It covers topics including:

- What was the challenge?
- What else did the case study subject try before?
- What results did they get before?
- What concerns did they have about trying the solution your client offers?
- What would have happened if they hadn't found a solution?
- Details of the product or service they used.

- Details of the results they got.
- What they'd say to anyone else contemplating using that product or service.

Why Do Businesses Need Case Studies?

Case studies are the equivalent of having your most satisfied customers, those with outstanding measurable results, line up to personally visit each of your prospects and share their success stories over coffee.

Minus the restraining orders that would undoubtedly follow from you trespassing in their living rooms.

Case studies allow you to capture these stories and send them to every one of your prospects.

A recent survey by MarketingProfs discovered 71% of Business-to-Business marketers use case studies as one of their most effective marketing tactics. This same survey showed that these B2B marketers believe case studies are the second most effective tactic they can use – only behind in-person events.

Creating great case studies isn't a walk in the park, if you don't know what you're doing. Here are just a few challenges businesses face – they're big enough to prevent most businesses from ever getting a finished case study published and working for them.

- Deciphering the key elements needed to make a compelling case study
- Finding the time to survey their customers to identify those who are having great success with their products and services
- Getting in touch with their most successful customers to interview them
- Getting their permission to use their name and their company name in the case study
- Knowing how to maximize the number of leads they can generate with them
- Taking someone off one of their current projects to create a case study

But, because they couldn't find a case study creation service, they get these headaches instead of great benefits:

- Without a steady stream of case studies getting leads is that much harder
- Without the influence case studies provide they have longer sales cycles
- Fewer leads will turn into sales without the social proof case studies provide

- If they don't provide great case studies, prospects will likely turn to their competitors who do provide case studies for their products and services

Think they might jump at the opportunity, if they could find the ideal solution for creating compelling case studies? That would include:

- Having someone outside of their business create case studies for them (this minimizes the interruptions to their already busy staff and existing projects)
- Have someone help track down their biggest client successes
- Have a well-defined plan and outline for creating compelling case studies
- Have someone set the appointment and interview their successful customers
- Have a great writer convert the interview into a compelling case study
- Have a strong call to action at the end of each case study so the prospect doesn't just smile and put down the case study without first taking the next step in the buying process

- Have someone help them maximize the use of case studies to get more leads and to nurture leads faster through the buying cycle
- Create a case study marketing plan to maximize the use of case studies throughout their business (i.e. website, leave behinds, mailing campaigns, etc.)
- Consistent branding, so their case study blends seamlessly with the rest of their marketing materials

The difference between the impact of an ordinary case study and a compelling case study is significant. A compelling case study attracts more readers, gives great clarity on the actual outcomes experienced by customers and gets the reader to identify with the subject of the case study, believing similar outcomes are possible for them.

Do Case Studies Help with SEO?

Yes! If you publish them on your client's site as well as in PDF and print form, you can get extra SEO mileage from this content. Especially if you count the other content you post that promotes the case study. Case study announcements make for excellent press releases, blog posts, videos, and more.

The ROI on Case Studies

There's a reason the case study is the darling of marketing firms everywhere. The reason is that social proof sells. In a marketplace filled with sheeple, nobody wants to be the first one in the buyer pool. We all want Mikey to taste the cereal first.

Case studies are the ideal way to convey: The water's fine! Come on in!

Many marketers have read the book Influence by Robert Cialdini. He's got another one called Yes!: 50 Secrets from the Science of Persuasion where he talks about a hotel chain that wanted to convince its guests to help them minimize the effect on the environment of washing every towel and sheet every day.

They first tested a generic placard message about helping save the environment. Then they changed the sign to say that the majority of people staying at that hotel participated in the program. The change increased participation by 26%. When they changed the sign again to state that the majority of people who had stayed in that particular room participated, participation increased by 33% over the standard message.

The more precisely you can match the person featured in the case study with the typical prospect, the more you will be able to influence their decision.

The more you publish case studies that hit the ball out of the park as far as letting your customers sell to your prospects, the more you'll sell.

How to Re-Sell Case Study Creation Services to Clients

1. Every business needs case studies. Here's how you recognize a good prospect for this service:

   - When you find business owners who are having trouble converting prospects into customers.

   - When you find business owners who have customers who've gotten remarkable, measurable results from using their product or service.

   - When you find clients who sell a product or service that prospects view with a measure of skepticism.

2. Ask probing questions to assess their need, and help them to see it, too:

   - How often do you produce and publish case studies of your remarkably successful customers?

   - How much hassle and time were involved in creating these case studies?

- How often do your prospects just disappear, and you sense if they'd only known they could really trust you to deliver what they need, that they would have bought?

3. Use a checklist to analyze their current case study plan with them:
   - Do they have any case studies?
   - Do they have any customers who'd be excellent candidates for profiling?
   - If they have case studies, are they written in a way that makes taking action an urgent and unquestionable response after reading?
   - Do they have a plan in place for promoting their case studies?
   - Do they have case studies planned that match up with the profile of each of their ideal customer types?

4. Communicate the benefits of professionally written case studies. Case studies can help them make more money by:
   - Using social proof to nudge prospects across the finish line by giving them a reason to believe what your product or service did for another, it will do for them, too.

- Decreasing the hands-on work of prospect follow-up.
- Subtly compelling readers to take action.
- Building credibility – the perception is that only 'real' businesses publish case studies.

5. Present a selection of done-for-you case study packages.

- Create your own case study creation packages by adding a margin to the packages of an outsource team.
- Give each package a name. You will find that if you offer three package levels, most clients will choose the middle package.
- For case study creation packages, you could make the quantity of case studies, creation of an editorial calendar, the level of done-for-you service in interviewing clients, or promotional services the distinguishing mark between pricing levels.
- Add this service into your marketing materials.
- Add done-for-you case studies to the list of services on your own website.

6. Order case study creation services for your client. Simply go to www.TriumphCom.com/nitro to order.

- Choose your package.
- Pay via PayPal.

- We will contact you to confirm receipt of your order and send you a questionnaire to complete on behalf of your client.
- We can either assemble information you provide, or handle everything from scheduling and interviewing the case study subject.
- We'll draft the text and send to you for approval.
- If revisions are needed, just let us know, and we'll get them done and back to you quickly.
- We can even create promotional content to help you get more mileage from the case study.

Sample Text for Your Website

What If Your Happiest Customers Became Your Best Salespeople?

Case studies harness the power of social proof to get your prospects to buy. It's far more effective to have a happy customer raving about your product or service than having a paid salesperson do it. When you create and publish case studies where your best customers share the outstanding, measurable results they got from doing business with you, your prospects listen without the skepticism that comes from watching a sales pitch.

But creating case studies isn't a quick and easy process... if you try it on your own. From knowing who to interview, what to ask, how to write it, and where to publicize your case study, this can be a big job.

That's why we offer done-for-you case studies. We take the headache and uncertainty out of the process so you can get all the benefits of higher conversion rates without the hassle.

Call or click to see why case studies are the second favorite marketing tool used by top marketing firms, and how they can work for your business, too.

This one content creation service alone can make an enormous difference for your clients – whether they sell products, services, or information – and for your bottom line as well. We not only make the case study creation process easy, it's also fun... but not nearly as much fun as when you start seeing conversion rates spike!

MMMM tasty!

better than
BACON?

b2b whitepapers: the never-ending feast

By Susan Anderson

Choice Words

Better than Bacon?
B2B Whitepapers: The Never-Ending Feast

Ever read that children's book "If You Give a Mouse a Cookie"? The gist is this… once you start feeding this greedy little rodent, he's going to own you. You'll be feeding him everything under the sun, waiting on him hand and foot, and pretty much catering to his every whim.

Or something like that.

Whitepapers are pretty much like that.

To put it another way. Think of your mom, girlfriend, wife… or yourself. What happens when there's a special event coming up? She goes out and buys a new outfit. The new outfit requires new shoes. The new shoes require a new purse. The new purse amplifies her need to have her nails done. And that means toes, too. Plus, now she's got to get a new lipstick that looks good with the nail polish. New lipstick is in close enough proximity to her earlobes that really, some new earrings aren't an unreasonable purchase. And of course, those new earrings come in a matched set with a new necklace. All that attention to her face, ears, and neck now make her need for a trim and touch up on her hair color. And now… she's done shopping. Until the next event.

Probably don't have to say much more, except that whitepapers are like that.

Semantics First: What Are Whitepapers?

Whitepapers are used by most businesses as a way to give their potential business clients education and information on a particular topic. They're generally used to help somebody make a decision. The most common areas of use are in politics, business and technical fields. In business, it's mostly for Business to Business (B2B) applications. B2B is the kind of business where their customers are businesses. So a management consultant's clients are other businesses. An office furniture store has customers that are primarily businesses. Much of the time these types of sales are a bit more complex than a person just walking into a store and buying a box of pens or a ream of paper...buying new office furniture will often involve the President, the CFO, the department manager and the facilities group in making a decision. Whitepapers serve as a way of getting everyone on the same page when it comes to solving a key problem your solution will fill.

A whitepaper acts as a report or guide. It focuses on a particular issue or problem and offers solutions. They can be used in politics, technical fields and in business. Often times they are used to highlight a specific product, but they may also be more general and cover the issues of large area. Whitepapers need to be very well written. They not only inform and educate business decision makers, but they persuade the audience of a specific point of view or solution. For example an eco-friendly cleaning company may have a whitepaper on the dangers of most common cleaning products. They will list how specific ingredients can cause problems with the environment and with people's health. At the end of the whitepaper, their products will be presented as a natural solution to the problem.

Whitepapers are more than simple brochures. The term comes from a white book which is an official government publication. Whitepapers carry more authority than a regular report or a marketing publication. They are informative, well researched and engaging.

They make the case for a specific solution to a problem. They can be used to introduce specific ways of thought, new technology, innovation and other products. Because of this, they are a natural fit for technology related issues. They help key decision-makers and influencers communicate their prescribed solutions, whether they are theoretical ideas or more practical applications.

In nearly every target market in a B2B environment, more than one person helps make the buying decision. There is typically an economic buyer (the one with the budget), a process buyer (the one in charge of integrating the purchased products or services into their business), and influencers (programmers, engineers, consultants, advisers - who can encourage or discourage the purchase).

If you were selling a salesforce automation system, the economic buyer might be the COO or CFO, the process buyer would be the sales manager, the influencers would be the top sales people, the IT manager, and maybe several from customer support.

If you go through the whole ROI analysis and try to get a customer service or IT person to read it, they will be gagging within seconds.

If you go through all of the improvements in productivity, shortening the sales cycle, and increasing average sales commissions, the customer service and IT people will be nodding off but the sales manager will devour every page.

If instead you talk about the database structure, the redundant hardware design, the role-based security systems and the data structure of the database tables, you'll have nearly everyone else tossing the whitepaper into the garbage can.

In a single whitepaper, it's nearly impossible to address each audience without boring the stew out of non-technical people, or going over their heads within a few paragraphs. They might pretend to keep reading, but all that's going through their minds is a film loop of Beavis (or was it Butthead?) reading aloud, "Words, words, uhhhh.... words…"

You may need several different versions of a whitepaper to reach the appropriate audiences for your product.

Why Do Businesses Need Whitepapers?
There are two main varieties of whitepapers. Government whitepapers are issued by the government and lay out policy or a proposed action on a very specific issue. Ehhh, we don't care about those, for our purposes.

Commercial whitepapers are what ought to have your local online marketer spidey senses tingling. These are marketing or sales tools that offer a specific solution, similar to the eco-friendly cleaning products example above. They can achieve a variety of different goals. This type of whitepaper can be used to generate sales leads, establish the company as a thought leader, make a business' case, or educate customers.

Within this category, there are three main types of commercial whitepapers.

- A business benefits paper makes the business case for a certain type of technology or methodology. These types of whitepapers are almost always marketing communications documents designed to promote a specific company's solutions or products. As a marketing tool, these papers will highlight information favorable to the company authorizing or sponsoring the paper. Such whitepapers are often used to generate sales leads, establish thought leadership, make a business case, or to educate customers.

- The technical paper describes how a certain technology works.

- A hybrid paper combines the two different varieties to include both business benefits and technical details into a single whitepaper.

Do Whitepapers Help with SEO?

Indirectly, yes. See, no whitepaper stands alone. Each one should have a landing page where you drive traffic and build a list by requiring an opt-in to get the whitepaper. The whitepaper itself is usually in secure PDF form, so the search engines don't see it... they just see whatever you put on the landing page and any marketing you do to drive traffic there.

Believe it or not, these decision makers are actively looking online for solutions. One study by MarketingProfs stated that 81% of engineers go online to conduct research on products.

Business buyers are online… and not just to play Candy Crush Saga. They've got lots of money to spend, and they're looking for the information decision makers need before they choose a solution.

The ROI on Whitepapers

Whitepapers can be used in a variety of different ways and there are many functions of whitepapers that your clients may have never heard of. You can help them get the most out of publishing whitepapers by suggesting they multi-purpose them like this:

- Whitepapers make a great source for informative PowerPoint presentations. By reformatting the text in the whitepaper, they can create a presentation to display on their website.

- Whitepapers can be given away on the company's website in exchange for email addresses. By giving away a whitepaper, your client can build their email marketing list and then send targeted messages to them in the future. Without a whitepaper that has a compelling title, a visitor would be less likely to opt-in to the prospect list. Which means after spending all that money to get a person to the site they will leave without your knowing who they are and without a chance to follow up with them. A good white paper with targeted traffic can often attract 20-30% of visitors to opt-in, dramatically increasing the number of qualified leads you get.

- White papers shorten the sales cycle. In complex sales the challenge is getting all of those involved in the buying decision on the same page. White papers get passed around to everyone influencing the decision and getting consensus much quicker.

- Whitepapers can also help with marketing because their release can trigger a widespread public relations campaign. When a whitepaper is released it is a big news event. It can spark blog posts, press releases, social media campaigns and a variety of other activities that can bring attention to a company. Be sure that your client is aware of these opportunities. You can offer the full slate of promotional content from press releases to blog posts to get the most out of their whitepaper's release.

How to Re-Sell Whitepaper Creation Services to Clients

1. Not every business needs whitepapers… but every B2B business does. Here's how you recognize a good prospect for this service:

    *   When you find B2B prospects who have a long sales cycle, involving a lot of lead nurturing.

    *   When you find B2B prospects who are already publishing white papers – but who might only be producing one white paper at a time hoping it will reach all the different decision makers involved.

    *   When you find B2B clients who want to take their prestige and expertise levels up a notch by positioning themselves as experts.

    *   Here's a short list of the types of businesses that need whitepapers: Business attorneys (corporate bankruptcy attorneys, contract lawyers, human resource attorneys, oil and gas attorneys, business attorneys, patent / intellectual property attorneys, product liability attorneys, tax attorneys, just to name a few), Software development companies, Management consultants, Accounting firms (especially dealing with the impact of Obamacare, and new tax laws and regulations, Ad agencies, Manufacturers, Commercial contractors, and Commercial builders

2. Ask probing questions to assess their need, and help them to see it, too:

- How often do you publish whitepapers?

- Each time you publish a whitepaper, how many versions do you create to target the various decision makers?

- When you've done whitepapers in the past, who did the research, the writing, and the promotion?

- How many new contacts opted in the last time you offered a whitepaper online?

- Did you have an autoresponder email message sequence to follow up with those leads?

- How did you promote the last whitepaper your company produced?

3. Use a checklist to analyze their current whitepaper inventory with them:

- A series of whitepapers is available on landing pages on their site so that people who opt in can download the whitepaper.

- Every whitepaper they produce has multiple versions to match the message and target audience well, using the most powerful language and jargon for each audience.

- Each whitepaper campaign also includes a series of autoresponder messages to nurture those leads.

- Each whitepaper features a truly compelling title that is practically irresistible to prospects.
- Each whitepaper includes a powerful call to action that spells out the next steps a reader should take.

4. Communicate the benefits of professionally written whitepapers. Whitepapers can help them make more money by:
   - Dripping your marketing message onto all of the B2B decision makers you consider prospects.
   - Decreasing some of the hands-on work of prospect follow-up.
   - Subtly compelling readers to take action.
   - Building credibility – the perception is that only 'real' businesses publish whitepapers.
   - Keeping prospects moving through a lengthy sales funnel by giving every decision maker involved the specific information they need to move forward.

5. Present a selection of done-for-you whitepaper packages.
   - Create your own whitepaper creation packages by adding a margin to the packages of an outsource team.

- Give each package a name. You will find that if you offer three package levels, most clients will choose the middle package.

- For whitepaper packages, you could make the quantity of whitepapers, creation of an editorial calendar, the source of the info (is a series of interviews involved?), or whitepaper promotion service the distinguishing mark between pricing levels.

- Add this service into your marketing materials.

- Add done-for-you whitepaper publishing to the list of services on your own website.

6. Order whitepaper creation services for your client. Simply go to www.TriumphCom.com/nitro to order.

- Choose your package.

- Pay via PayPal.

- We will contact you to confirm receipt of your order and send you a questionnaire to complete on behalf of your client.

- If you prefer, for an additional fee, we can interview you or your client to extract that information (painless, we promise!) without you having to complete the questionnaire.

- We'll draft the text based on what you've approved, and send to you for final approval within a month or less, in most cases.

- If revisions are needed, just let us know, and we'll get them done and back to you quickly.

- We can handle repurposing the contents and creating the promotional content to complete the project for you, including press releases, autoresponder messages, and blog posts, for an additional fee.

Sample Text for Your Website

B2B's: Ready to Inform, Educate and Persuade Your Audience?
A Professionally-Written Whitepaper Does It All
Whitepapers are one of the most powerful sales and marketing tools available for B2B marketing. When you use whitepapers to market your products or services you'll experience:

- Increased sales
- Increased lead generation
- Increased customer trust and confidence
- An advantage in your marketplace
- A significant return on your investment

Writing a whitepaper that engages the audience and informs them of your product or service can be difficult without the right writing skills. That's where professional whitepaper creation services come in. Following proven whitepaper creation methods can get your company the right kind of attention.

Whitepapers require in-depth research, accurate reporting and the use of statistical data. It's not promotional or hyped up. Your whitepaper should position your company in the right light with persuasive, engaging and informative writing.

Contact us today for a whitepaper that makes an impact.

They say that working for clients who pay you tens of thousands of dollars a month is just as easy (maybe more so!) as working for a client who's only paying you a hundred bucks. Whitepapers are the perfect illustration of this principle at work. If you land B2B clients who swim with the big boys, the sheer volume and variety of whitepapers you could create for them to help them make more sales should put a smile on your face.

Have We Gotta Deal for You!

That wraps up details on the top ten content creation projects we do for clients – projects you need for your business, and your clients need for their businesses. As your top secret white label content creation machine, we're delighted to have the opportunity to partner with you and make you more money while simultaneously contributing top-notch content to the online world.

Speaking of which, how's this for a deal?

It will help me tremendously to get feedback from you. But you're busy, I know! So how about this…

If you loved this book, found it helpful, or at least laughed at all the right places, please go onto Amazon, search for this book, and leave a 4-5 star review and comments that will help other local online marketers realize their lives will never be complete without reading this book. Then, send me an email letting me know you did this very good deed. Here's the email address: sue@triumphcom.com

OR…

If you are reaching for your bottle of Tums because even your stomach hates this book, you think it's the worst piece of drivel ever chiseled, and you're halfway thinking about tripping me in the hall if we meet, instead, please send me an email detailing just how bad your experience reading this book was, what you hated most, and what slimy creature you'd rather kiss than read it again. Here's the email address: sue@triumphcom.com

Either way, I'd like to offer you 10% off your first order with Triumph.

About the Author

Susan Anderson... Sue LaPointe – no big difference. She'll answer to both, but even if you knew her before, if you really want to look like you're up on current events, you'll make the switch she's making to her maiden name: Susan Anderson.

'Nuff said about that.

Susan's the owner of Triumph Communications, LLC, a freelance commercial writing firm based out of, well, wherever she happens to be at the moment (Huntsville, Alabama). Her hand-picked team of U.S. based writers and project managers have served hundreds of clients and completed thousands of projects since 2005.

An avid Internet marketing student (yes, that's a polite way of saying a course junkie), Susan has worked with Nitro Marketing since 2008, including a stint as VP Design and Development in the early days of Local Business Money Machine's creation. She is also the editor-in-chief of the monthly newsletter of the Local Internet Marketing Association.

Mom to two teens and an old dog, she counts walking on fire and breaking a wooden arrow with her throat as piece-of-cake kinds of accomplishments in comparison.

You can reach her here:
sue@triumphcom.com
www.TriumphCom.com/nitro